Lost in Space² and Found

Blast Off into the Expanded Edition

By Angela Cartwright and Bill Mumy

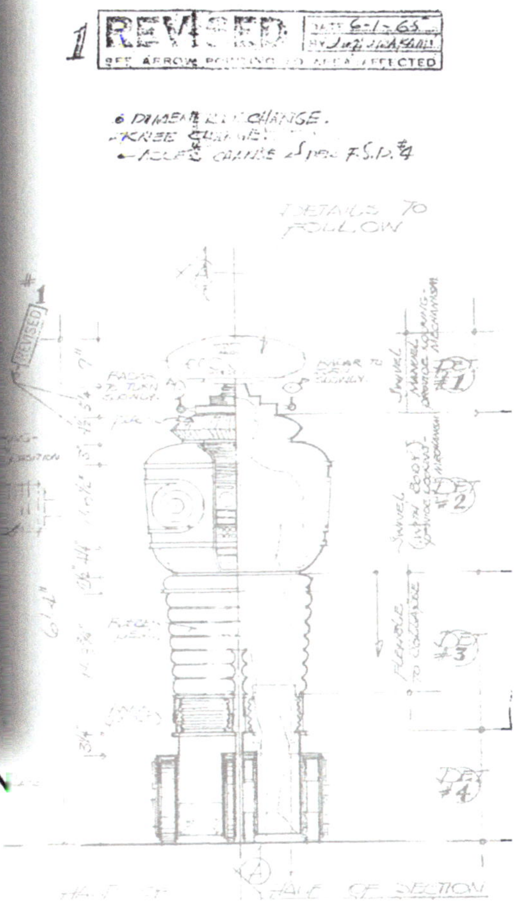

LOST (AND FOUND) IN SPACE² : BLAST OFF INTO THE EXPANDED EDITION

Lost in Space® and its characters and designs are © Legend Pictures, LLC.
Licensed by Synthesis Entertainment. Copyright © 2021 Synthesis Entertainment.
All rights reserved.

Published by Next Chapter Publishing. This book or any portion thereof may not be reproduced or used in any manner whatsoever without the express written permission of the publisher.

For permissions or for bulk sales, contact the publisher at requests@ncpbooks.com.

All photos in this book (except where otherwise credited) are © Legend Pictures, LLC.

ISBN: 978-1-7356215-3-1

Publication date: September 14, 2021

Next Chapter Publishing
A Division of Next Chapter Entertainment LLC
Los Angeles, California

Publishers: Mary McLaren
Tom McLaren

nextchapterent.com   ncpbooks.com

INTRODUCTION

"Once upon a time we were young kids embarking on a quest that would take us into deep space and unknown alien worlds where danger and excitement awaited us every week for three years. And now, more than half a century later, the story continues.

It's interesting how images can be portals to files in the mind locked away long ago. Creating this book together opened a floodgate of happy memories.

Several years after our first edition of this book was published, Kevin Burns called us into his office and handed over copies of hundreds of newly acquired *Lost in Space* photographs from the CBS network archive that had not been seen since the show first went off the air. He was very excited about it all, and told us we had full access to his files should we want to update our *Lost in Space* book.

It seemed only right with so many additional events and remembrances that we revisit, revise, and expand the book. We have added more than 600 new images and over 160 brand new pages.

Along the way we were able to relive so many cherished moments and reflect upon the fact that this diverse group of actors, who came together for the first time on the set, somehow melded their own personalities with the scripted characters and became a true family.

A family that continues to love each other to this day, more than half a century later.

A family whose work continues to bring pleasure and joy to a world that needs it now more than ever.

We are grateful and proud to be part of that family and are blessed to be a part of such an iconic project that has brought so much joy to so many over the last 50+ years. Our hope is these found photographs and stories connect the reader to a simpler and magical time."

Angela

"Experiencing something like co-starring in a hit television series as children together was a pretty big and life-altering deal. Ange and I were both seasoned professional actors when we started working alongside each other on *Lost in Space* and of course we went through several years of growing, joined at the hip. But the continued success and lifespan of the series was not something we could ever have imagined.

How strange to know that something you were a part of well over 50 years ago has resonated nonstop all around the world. *Lost in Space* has been translated and dubbed into many different languages and seen in many different cultures and the show has influenced countless career choices over the decades.

How strange to realize people continue to think of you as children.

Young minds are like sponges and they soak up their environment differently than a fully developed adult brain does. It's the prefrontal cortex in its early growth, I suppose. But I can say this much with total assurance: I recall my experiences working on *Lost in Space* as a youth much clearer than I recall my experiences of working on other projects, like *Babylon 5*, as an adult. The relationships that were formed during our years filming the series have proven to be true family ties that bind.

Ange and I agreed that a photographic memoir of the series, commemorating the 50th anniversary, was a good and worthy idea. We put the first edition of this book together basically the same way one would put a photo scrapbook together. A few shared details, memories, dates, and circumstances that only we knew accompanied the rare and unseen images we picked to celebrate the much-loved show. But, returning to it again six years later, with a lot of new water under our 'Lost in Space bridge,' we felt that sharing the deeper stories, the true childhood impressions and emotional memories, and yes, the secrets (many of them anyway, but not ALL) would be the focus of this expanded edition. And, expanded it most definitely is!

How strange to be labeled as 'senior citizens' now, both of us grandparents, and yet here we are, continuing to reflect on those treasured childhood years we shared working together on the series. No one but us has the unique perspective we have on the experiences of being lost (and found) in space together.

How strange indeed."

LET'S START AT THE VERY BEGINNING...

December 1964:

The Beatles' *I Feel Fine* was topping the pop charts;
President Lyndon Johnson was escalating the bombing in Vietnam;
Goldfinger was the big movie of the month;
Angela Cartwright and Billy Mumy were cast as Penny and Will Robinson in Irwin Allen's ambitious pilot for 20th Century Fox, *Lost in Space*.

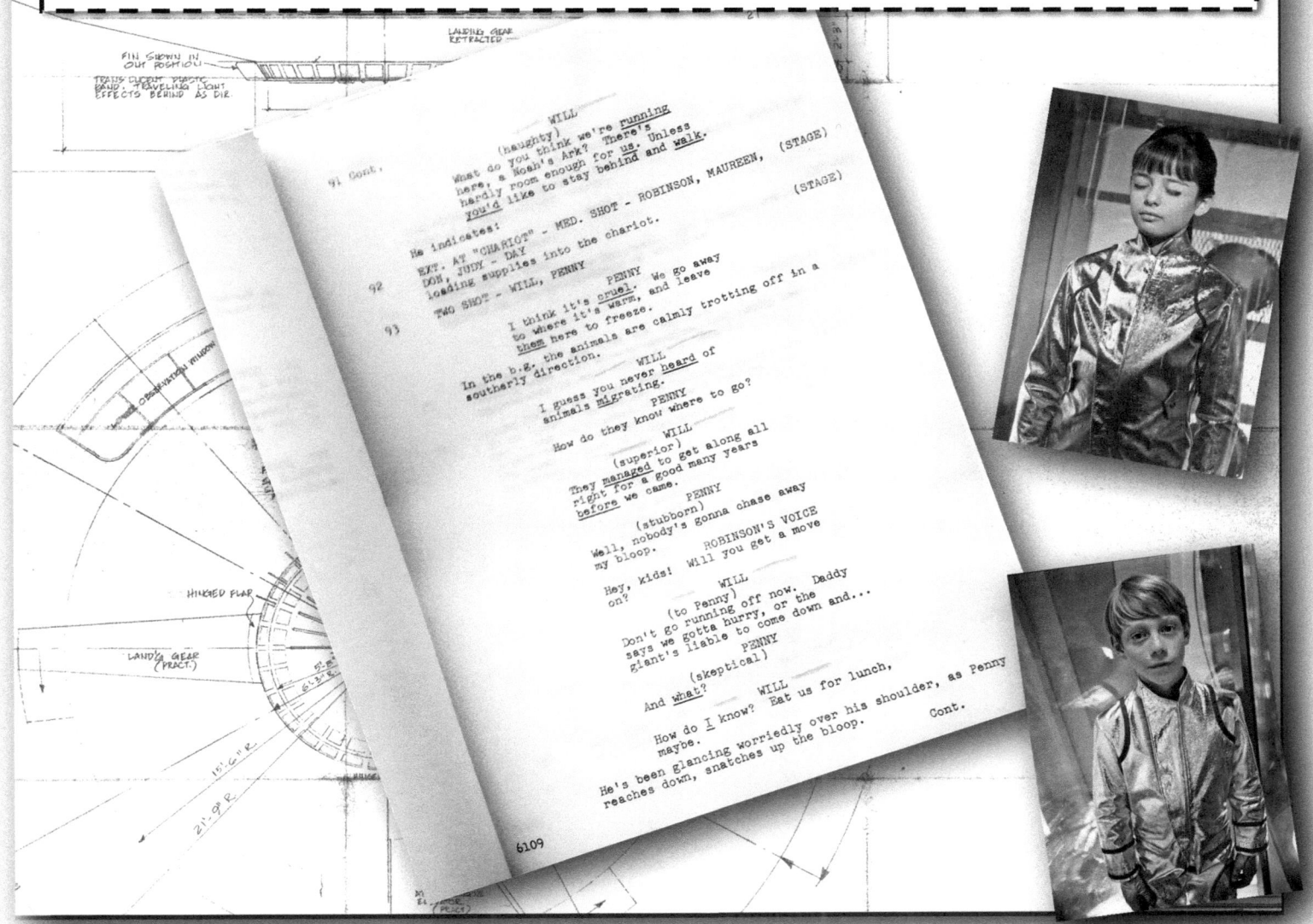

BLAST OFF!

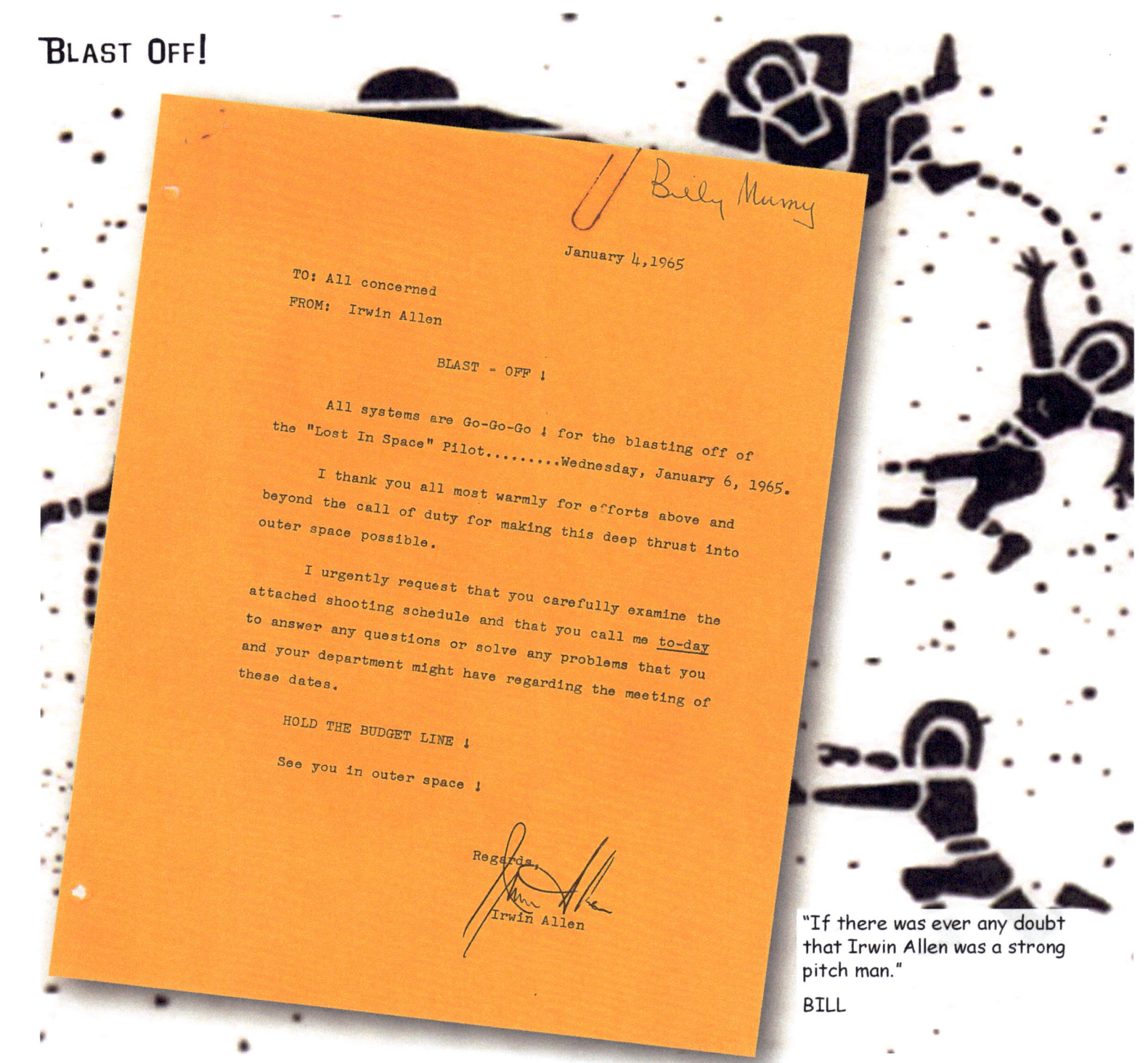

Billy Mumy

January 4, 1965

TO: All concerned
FROM: Irwin Allen

BLAST - OFF !

All systems are Go-Go-Go ! for the blasting off of the "Lost In Space" Pilot.........Wednesday, January 6, 1965.

I thank you all most warmly for efforts above and beyond the call of duty for making this deep thrust into outer space possible.

I urgently request that you carefully examine the attached shooting schedule and that you call me <u>to-day</u> to answer any questions or solve any problems that you and your department might have regarding the meeting of these dates.

HOLD THE BUDGET LINE !

See you in outer space !

Regards,
Irwin Allen

"If there was ever any doubt that Irwin Allen was a strong pitch man."

BILL

FYI In preparation there were hair and wardrobe fittings on the 20th Century Fox lot and revised scripts arriving in the mail with new colored pages. All was ready for shooting to begin on January 6, 1965.

"Irwin Allen's original vision for Lost in Space was an action-packed, full of adventure, family journey into the unknown. He directed the pilot himself (which was the most expensive TV pilot ever produced for television up to that time), He created a really strong template that served us well."
BILL

"On the first day of filming the Lost In Space pilot I found this handwritten note from Irwin waiting for me in my dressing room. A very nice way to start my space adventures."
ANGELA

"There were many technical moving parts to create before the actors set foot on the stage. Sets needed to be built, aliens envisioned. Irwin had a dream and he gathered some of the best in the business to make it happen. Imaginations were plucked."
ANGELA

"Filming the pilot was so much fun! Everyone had a blast. Literally. Everyday we shot new action sequences. We struggled to stand still and keep our eyes closed inside the freezing tubes while the special effects crew detonated explosion after explosion around us all on the upper deck of the Jupiter 2. Sparks, smoke, and flames combusted while we pretended to be sleeping human popsicles."
BILL

"The second unit shot the actual jet pack scenes. The jet pack really worked and was piloted by the only guy that has ever flown this JPL jet pack. Shot in Red Rock Canyon in the Mojave Desert. The only time the production left the 20th Century Fox lot."
ANGELA

"The spacewalk scene was filmed on Stage 11 with Guy challenging the vacuum of deep space.

Bill and I loved filming the anti-gravity segment where we floated around the upper deck of the Jupiter 2. The harnesses we had to wear were extremely uncomfortable, but it was worth it. I thought it was funny how they had tied my ponytail up with a wire so it looked like it was floating. I've always loved attention to the details."
ANGELA

Space Family Robinson

"This picture explains the Robinson family so well... Maureen has eyes for her hubby John, Will and Penny converse and annoy each other in the back of the chariot, Judy is flirting with Don. John is seriously protecting his family. And Don is not paying attention to what he's doing which explains his nickname Crash West."
ANGELA

"We truly bonded as a family while filming the chariot scenes. In between takes we would play Password and other games. We were inside that vehicle for hours at a time, sometimes drenched to the bone. It was like a family vacation in the weirdest way possible."
BILL

FYI The chariot was a fully functional multi-terrain vehicle. It was built by the Fox prop department on top of a Sno-Cat.

"I remember how much fun Bill and I had in that chariot. And we were in it shooting for hours at a time. We couldn't wait until they opened the hatch and dumped torrents of water on our heads. We were bounced around in the chariot endlessly. It's hard to believe June and Guy are smiling here, perhaps they had just announced that it was a wrap!"
ANGELA

WET AND WILD

"For the crossing the sea sequences, the chariot was put on a gimble, and off camera, several crew members heaved and put their backs into making that heavy vehicle filled with six people and a chimpanzee rock back and forth like a teeter totter from hell. They dumped countless gallons of water on us for days. Ange and I, typical kids, loved getting as wet as possible. We all were drenched and we all laughed like maniacs."
BILL

"As we were looking through these images from the pilot both Bill and I said how we wished Irwin Allen had directed more episodes. He did such a great job."
ANGELA

"Ange looks somewhat Kryptonian in this photo to me."
BILL

Expedition Unknown

"The ancient alien ruins set was a masterpiece. It looked fantastic. We were on that set for a few days. That's the first time we splintered off into separate groups. Ange and I filmed our bit in the alien mummy tomb. They created giant spider webs all around us that were made out of rubber cement.
I think that was the first time Penny Robinson screamed. That gal has some pipes."
BILL

"Don't think for one second that I wasn't well aware that Ange was grabbing my thigh."
BILL

"The earthquake in the ancient alien section was a huge scene for the pilot. There were special effects, rubber rocks being thrown at us, shaking walls, and it took hours to set up the shot. You could feel the tension on the set as everyone prepared for what they hoped would be one take only. While the cameras began to roll and Irwin yelled 'ACTION,' Guy and June rocked and rolled their way to the wall fighting their way through rocks and cobwebs. And then Guy heard our voices trapped behind the wall and he pulled out his laser gun and cut a hole to free us... but he forgot to turn the laser gun light off, and he shot each one of us as we climbed through the wall to freedom.
'Cut! Reset!' Swear words were muttered. A couple of hours later we reshot the scene. That was a tough day for Irwin Allen."
ANGELA

Launching the Three Year Adventure

"We started filming *The Reluctant Stowaway* on July 19, 1965. I remember the date because it was my mother's birthday. What I recall most about it was Mark had just suffered a pretty serious motorcycle accident and he was very sore and bruised and getting into the heavy scratchy silver spacesuit was quite painful for him.

I thought adding the Robot and Dr. Smith to the series were great ideas from the beginning. Editing the pilot into the first five episodes was smart and worked out very well. It took a few months and several episodes before it was obvious to me that the tone of the pilot was not going to be the final tone of the series."
BILL

Cast Of Characters

> **FYI** Note the Robot's claws are silver. When we went to color in Season 2, they were painted red.

"Here we are: the Robinsons, Major West, Dr. Smith, and the Robot B-9 on the upper deck of the Jupiter 2. Note the ceiling is uncovered so the cinematographer could light the set. This photo was taken in July 1965."
BILL

"The Robinson siblings pretty much covered the spectrum of hair colors."
BILL

GUY WILLIAMS AS PROFESSOR JOHN ROBINSON

TV COMMENTATOR
Heading the expedition will be Doctor John Robinson, Professor of Astrophysics at the University of Stellar Dynamics, now seen on your screen.

Guy Williams: a Sicilian Renaissance man, sophisticated, brilliant father of two, actor-model turned iconic action hero superstar, a class act all the way. Strong, smart and brave. Someone you'd want to lead you through the darkness and tell you a joke as he did it. A real old-time Hollywood leading man with the looks, brains, and charisma to back it up.

"Guy was physical and compelling, with a warm, fuzzy, kind interior. He loved opera and fine wine, two things we did not have in common at the time. I had never watched Zorro so I didn't know him from the roles he had played. I just knew him as Guy, my space dad."
ANGELA

"Guy Williams, as Zorro, along with George Reeves as Superman, was the main reason I wanted to become an actor and get inside the TV as a four year old kid. By the time we started *Lost in Space*, I'd been acting professionally over half my life, alongside some truly iconic stars, but working with Guy was a real treat for me. He was a very impressive human specimen. He was tall, strong, smart, magnetic, confident, handsome as all hell, and a truly caring nice man. I loved the father-son scenes we shared together."
BILL

JUNE LOCKHART AS DR. MAUREEN ROBINSON

June Lockhart: second generation showbiz aristocracy, cut her teeth performing on Broadway, ingénue turned into a very successful safety zone mom for America's TV viewers, with a razor-sharp mind like a sponge and the desire to bring those around her up to her level. A deceptively rebellious bold soul in the shell of comfort and pioneer spirit. A powerful blend of practicality and passion.

"June is a brilliant woman. Super smart. She devoured books and newspapers like I devoured cheese and crackers. June kept our fertile young minds awake by playing word games with me and Ange whenever there was a lull in filming and we weren't in school. Password, Scrabble, Boggle. What people don't really know about her is she's a rock 'n' roll gal. Truly. They think of her as this perfect, traditional, family values mother on television. But June is a bold and rebellious rocker."
BILL

```
                    COMMENTATOR'S VOICE
                (filter)
            ...With him, marking the first time
            in history that anyone but an adult
            male has passed the International
            Space Administration's gruelling
            physical and emotional screening
            for intergalactic flight, will be...

11      CLOSE SHOT - MAUREEN                          (STAGE)
        A brilliant woman of thirty-five, of sturdy   (TRANS-LIGHT
        Western pioneer stock, yet possibly just a little  BACKING)
        too maternal and feminine for the adventures and
        ordeals in store.  Trying hard to control her feeling of
        trepidation, she steps into one of the narrow tubes.
        CLOSE IN on her momentarily frightened but trusting eyes,
        as Robinson kisses her good-bye with intense feeling.
        The tube automatically locks airtight, and instantly fills
        with a dazzling light.  ZOOM IN on Maureen's eerily frozen
        face in suspended animation.  Simultaneously:

                    COMMENTATOR'S VOICE
                (filter)
            ...His wife, Doctor Maureen Robinson,
            the distinguished biochemist of the
            New Mexico College of Space Medicine...
```

"Wordsmith… game player…
yoga enthusiast… extremely
intelligent with a wicked sense of
humor and a very distinctive laugh.
Every year since I have known June
she has sent birthday and Christmas
card wishes to me and my family.
June loved a good time. She
always knew what was going
on in the world and in outer space
thanks to her voracious reading
habits and NASA contacts. In my
opinion she was a perfect Maureen
Robinson. Strong, wise, smart.
America's favorite mom is a
potpourri of contradictions."
ANGELA

MARK GODDARD AS MAJOR DON WEST

> 12 Cont.
>
> with honors in Celestial Geology and the measurement of synchroton radiation, Don moves encouragingly to help Judy into the tube, and Robinson, slightly amused, acknowledges that he has ceased to be The Man in his daughter's life.

Mark Goddard: the man-child from Massachusetts who leaps before looking. Impulsive, cocky, handsome as anyone can ever be, and constantly reminded of that fact. Mark was only 29 when cast in the series, and he had three previous network series under his belt already. He had a beautiful wife connected to the power-making decisions of showbiz, an infant daughter, a home in Beverly Hills, and the respect of his peers, like Steve McQueen. He was funny and fearless and riding the big new wave of the psychedelic 1960s like a champion surfer. And whenever he wiped out, he quickly grabbed his board and leapt back into the punishing and rewarding waters.

"Mark is a real character. He's a great actor and a very, very funny guy. I always thought of Mark as a big brother in a way, but in another way, I thought of him as a younger brother. He and I got into some serious troublemaking once in awhile on the lot and off the lot. I'm sure they found at least one or two golf carts at the bottom of the lake on the backlot when they dredged it!"
BILL

```
14   CLOSE SHOT - ROBINSON                    (STAGE)
     smiles proudly. Then, with the briefest ,  (TRANS-LIGHT
     flicker of anxiety in his eyes, watches them   BACKING)
     being automatically sealed and quick-frozen.
     PAN WITH HIM passing the other tubes, in which Judy already
     stands frozen, and Don has now positioned himself, giving
     us our first full view of his dark, intense, rugged features.
                    COMMENTATOR'S VOICE
                         (filter)
               Their assistant, Doctor Donald West,
               graduate student at the Center for
               Radio Astronomy, is the same young
               man who, last year, rocked the
               scientific world with his theory,
               since amply confirmed, that a planet's
               fitness for human habitation can be
               determined solely from the wave length
               and gyrofrequency of its reflected
               radar emissions.
```

"Mark always makes me laugh and I always enjoyed his antics. He was like a mischievous boy in a man's body. To this day I marvel at his quick wit. He's one of a kind and so very handsome. Which is why in *The Epilogue*, the final chapter of the Robinsons' adventures, I could see Penny having a fling with Don West. After all, the Robinsons were only human and who could resist those knee high boots and mini skirts after so long in outer space!"
ANGELA

MARTA KRISTEN AS JUDY ROBINSON

                    COMMENTATOR'S VOICE
           (filter)
    ...Their daughter, Judith, age nine-
    teen, who has rather heroically
    postponed all hopes for a career in
    the musical comedy field for the next
    two centuries at least.

Marta Kristen: the breathtakingly gorgeous orphan from Norway. Shuffled to the states as a little girl and discovered and tossed into showbiz like something out of a Shirley Temple story. Naive, open, loving, very sensitive, and very young, Marta found solace on the *Lost in Space* set, where she could be safe and away from a tough marriage, she longed for a family like the Robinsons. Her vulnerable beauty affected all who saw her.

"Marta was like a big sister to me. Because she was a married woman and I was just a kid we didn't really become friends until my adult years. We found a common thread in both loving art and music. We've shared many laughs and stories over drinks and a meal. We don't always agree on our take on life... but I think we respect each other's point of view."
ANGELA

"Marta, what a beauty. Such a sweet soul, with more than a touch of sadness about her. Marta was in a very tough marriage when we were shooting *Lost in Space*. I think she found solace in the sanctuary of the soundstages away from reality prime. She turned me on to some great music in the mid-1960s - Bob Dylan and The Byrds, to name two. She and I used to sit and sing harmony together while I played guitar. Our version of The Kingston Trio's arrangement of *Sloop John B*, made it into an episode. Brian Wilson reinvented the song around that time for the Beach Boys classic *Pet Sounds* album."
BILL

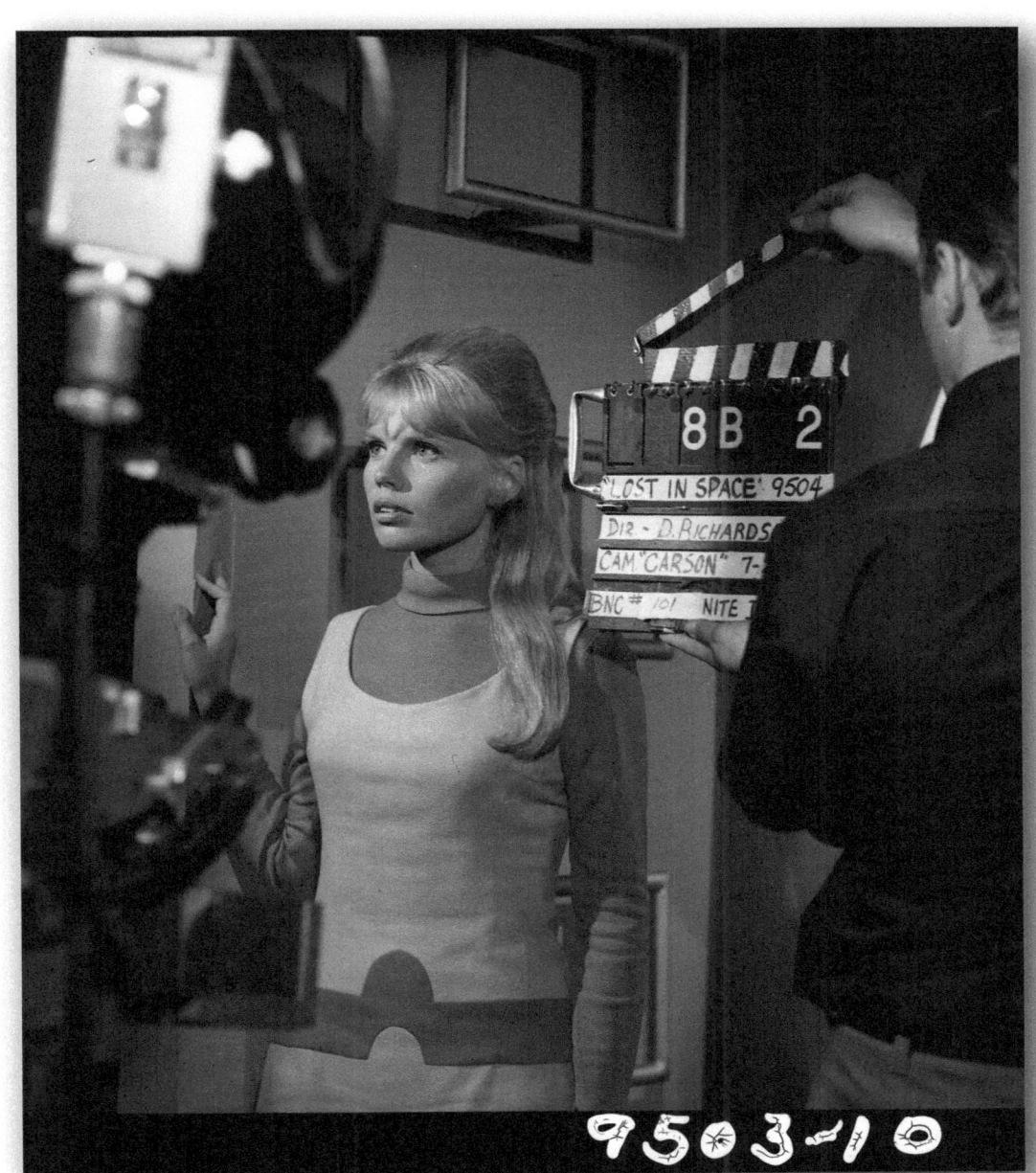

BILLY MUMY AS WILL ROBINSON

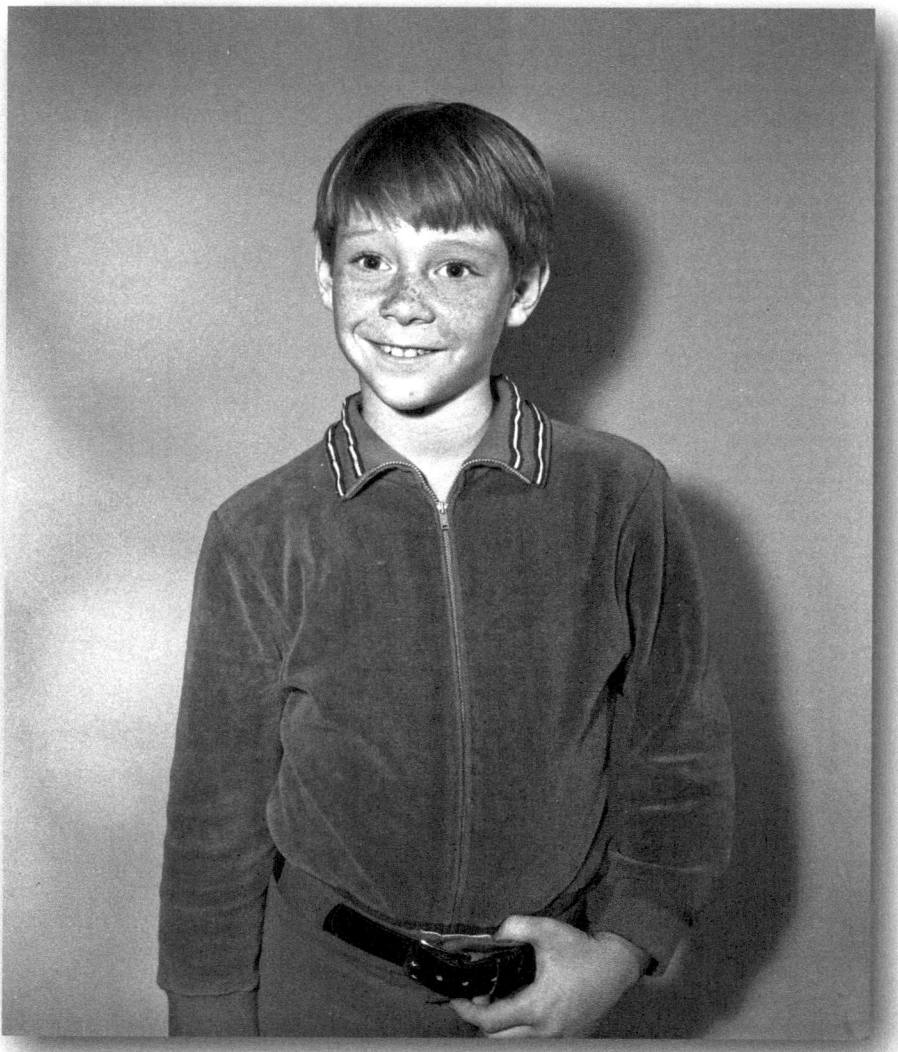

> Billy Mumy: that all-American, freckle-faced, red-haired kid who could believably play any type of character and pretty much had by the time *Lost in Space* started. A local, born and raised in Los Angeles around the studios, he'd spent half his life working alongside the biggest and greatest talents in Hollywood history before signing on to play genius superhero Will Robinson. When the camera rolled, Mumy always believed what he was doing. And that made the kids watching on TV believe it as well.

"Bill had done some pretty impressive work before he was cast as Will Robinson. Once you saw that little boy 'wish you into the cornfield' it was a hard image to get out of your head. Who hadn't seen Bill in the *Twilight Zone* or any of the plethora of other roles he had starred in before he embraced the role of Will Robinson? Right from the beginning he slipped into the Will character like it was an old slipper. Bill was meant to play that role and he did so with his heart and soul. He had a ton of dialogue to learn and he was good. He was real good. Cute as can be too with his red hair and freckles. Bill is also mega talented in other ways, like writing songs, playing the guitar, and drawing his comic books. He is funny and quirky and sometimes frustrating. We got along great from the get go on the set and off. Our friendship has remained special to me since the day we met."
ANGELA

```
13      TWO SHOT - WILL AND PENNY                              (STAGE)
        WILL, twelve, already is a whiz at electronics, (TRANS-LIGHT
        and one of those rare bookworms who can more than    BACKING)
        hold his own on a football field.

                        COMMENTATOR'S VOICE
                    (filter)
                Their son, Will, who recently was
                graduated from the Camdo Canyon
                School of Science at the age of
                nine, with the highest average
                in the school's history...And
                their daughter Penny, age eleven;
                I.Q., 147; hobby, zoology.
```

"Of all the characters I've ever played, Will Robinson is my all-time favorite. He could fly the ship. He could program the robot. He was a good shot with a laser gun. He always seemed to get into trouble and then get everyone out of trouble. He was a little superhero and that's exactly why I wanted to go into the acting world in the first place... to be a superhero."
BILL

Danger, Will Robinson!

Angela Cartwright as Penny Robinson

PENNY now joins Will in quickly entering her allotted tube, without waiting to be helped or encouraged. Penny, a quick-witted tomboy who attracts danger like a magnet, has read everything ever written by Jules Verne, and will never in her life forgive Mr. Lewis Carroll for not having written at least one hundred sequels to "Alice In Wonderland".

Angela Cartwright: the seasoned pro who had already done it all by the time the pilot started. Nothing could rattle her. She was born in ravaged and rationed England just seven years after World War II ended. She was tough and happy. Still is. She was always ready. She grew from a little girl into an incredibly gorgeous young woman before the TV audience's eyes, each week the progression became more stunning. Smart, secretive, and bold. Steady on.

"Ange was showbiz royalty by the time we started *Lost in Space*. Everyone watched *The Danny Thomas Show* every week and she'd had a seven year run on that series, growing up from a literal toddler in front of America in black and white. Ange went straight from playing Linda Williams on her long-running hit series into *The Sound of Music* as Brigitta von Trapp. While she was co-starring in that 20th Century Fox feature film, I was co-starring in a different Fox feature, *Dear Brigitte*, with Jimmy Stewart and Brigitte Bardot. Too bad that Ange's film kinda slipped through the cracks and didn't resonate like mine did... Gadzooks! We both went directly into *Lost in Space* after we wrapped up *Dear Brigitte* and, what's that other one called again? Oh yeah, *The Sound of Music*. Maybe some of you might remember that one."
BILL

"Penny was supposed to be a zoologist and they showed that in the early episodes of the show. I loved that about my character. A young girl genius interested in various forms of animal life that she would encounter on her travels in space to places unknown. Pretty sure that captured some people's imaginations, it sure captured mine."
ANGELA

JONATHAN HARRIS AS DR. ZACHARY SMITH

Jonathan Harris: born in the Bronx, he grew up so poor he had to sleep on the dining room table because his family had to rent out his room to make ends meet. A man so strong of will that he completely reinvented himself to serve his destiny. He became a man of high class and character. It wasn't an act. This larger-than-life 'late comer' to the show became the star by creating a character and a formula the fans and the network loved to hate. Jonathan was grateful and absolutely loved his time on the set. A consummate professional actor who never forgot how lucky he was to have the gig.

"Jonathan joined our cast and quickly became the Alpha Dog. But he was always gracious, charming, sweet as can be, totally prepared, and full of joy. He absolutely loved being Dr. Zachary Smith, and he and I had undeniable chemistry together. Although, I felt many times that the show was getting way too silly, I always had fun acting opposite Jonathan. We laughed a lot. I'm glad to say we were good friends. I miss him all the time."
BILL

15 CLOSE SHOT - SMITH
SMITH is a stocky, intelligent-looking man in his forties with a Long John Silver type of charm. He wears a phosphorescent, high-security clearance badge on his U. S. Space Corps coveralls. As he looks around, his eyes light on something o.s. and he grins quizzically.

"I've worked with my share of unprofessional actors, but Jonathan was never one of them. Always enthusiastic and prepared with the huge amount of dialogue had had to say (most of which he had written himself the night before), Jonathan was a pleasure to work with day in and day out.
Jonathan reimagined the character of Dr. Smith and what a memorable character he was. He got such a kick out of some of the lines he would say and murmur aside, 'how silly is this line?' Then Jonathan would giggle. He was so grateful for the chance to play a role week after week that he truly loved. He was very grateful indeed!"
ANGELA

Bob May as the Robot

"Bobby May was the hardest working guy in showbiz. Very enthusiastic about everything. He was a constant cheerleader. He painted his chair silver. He painted the inside of his dressing room silver. Bobby took a couple of serious tumbles inside the robot during our years of filming, but he never complained. He never had a bad word to say about anyone on the show. I remember the day his son, Marty, was being born. Bobby wanted to stay on the set to deliver off-camera dialogue while they were shooting a close-up of me. Everyone ordered him to get to the hospital. He left wearing the black face makeup!"
BILL

FYI We were told not to tell anyone that there was a man inside the robot, and it was years before the truth came out.

16 P.O.V. SHOT - THE ROBOT
This seven-foot-high electronic marvel is bedecked in shimmering aluminum coils topped by a magnificent glass head encasing electronic eyes and other sensors. The great Robot stands immobile on a thick plastic disc -- A dim light from beneath the Robot's feet casts weird, unearthly shadows on the massive torso. The intermittent light reveals a broad, circular aluminum plate supported by a gleaming tube which extends from the ceiling to hold the Robot immobile. The power-pak unit is in the Robot's side.

"Bobby May took his job very seriously. There was no larking around when he had his B-9 costume on. You could not have chosen a better or more willing guy to put inside that hot suit for 12 hours a day. He was totally committed, totally serious, totally in love with being the Robot."
ANGELA

Dick Tufeld as the Robot Voice

"Dick Tufeld worked on every single episode of *Lost In Space*, yet the cast never met him in person until the 1990s. Dick recorded his voice-over Robot dialogue in a post recording studio on the lot, not on the Fox soundstages where we filmed. Bobby May figured out little ways to give character to the Robot prop and he was great inside that dangerous cramped suit. Bobby memorized and delivered all the Robot's dialogue, but of course it sounded like it came from inside a fiberglass box, so the Robot's voice was re-recorded by the mighty Dick Tufeld. Dick had an amazing tonality and his Robot voice was perfect. Dick was a nice, smart, hip, jazz aficionado. He was close friends with Miles Davis. Cool, indeed."
BILL

DEBBIE AS THE BLOOP

"I enjoyed my scenes with Debbie. She was sweet and we really grew to love and trust one another. I was so sad when she disappeared from the show in Season 3. None of my doing, that is for sure."
ANGELA

Johnny Williams

"We were so fortunate to have a young talented composer named Johnny Williams write our themes. I think the pieces he created for *Lost In Space* still resonate as some of his finest music. He changed his billing to 'John' afterwards and did pretty good in showbiz. You may have heard of him."
BILL

"I love how we all had our own themes. There was Dad and Will music, Robot music, Penny exploring music, and of course Robot and Dr. Smith music. Those themes wove the fabric of the show and made each episode distinctive in such an amazing way."
ANGELA

Behind the Curtain

"Here's what shooting a scene on *Lost in Space* was REALLY like... imagine we have just finished a dress rehearsal and the scene involves the entire cast. The scene is blocked, lit, and floor marks are buried and disguised so not to be obvious. Makeup and hair departments are powdering and combing the actors and wardrobe folks are removing tissues from our collars, zipping zippers, adjusting buckles, and lining up trim on costumes. The effects crew begins spraying smoke or watering down the sand or spraying down plastics to matte out reflections. The upper 'bubble' is locked into place on the Robot and Bobby is no longer visible...

DIRECTOR: 'Time is money. Let's shoot this.'
CINEMATOGRAPHER: 'Back to one!' (The camera and the lighting return to their starting positions.)
ASSISTANT DIRECTOR: (loudly to all) 'This will be picture, people! Put us on a bell!' (The stage manager pushes a button and an elongated single note electronic 'bell-buzzer' can be heard throughout the enormous soundstage. Flashing red lights at all stage doors, interior and exterior, are illuminated.)
ASSISTANT DIRECTOR: 'Kill the fans and AC! Settle down, folks!' (The air conditioning system and large fans to keep the set cool are switched off. The noise level decreases greatly.)
ASSISTANT DIRECTOR: 'Picture up!'
CAMERA OPERATOR: 'We're rolling.'
SOUND MAN: 'Sound is rolling. Speed.'
JUNE: (to Angela and Marta, but we all take heed) 'Tits and Lips!' (Meaning: wet your lips and stand up straight, presenting your best posture.)
CAMERA ASSISTANT: (holds clapboard with scene info up in front of camera and loudly speaks) 'Scene 22B, Take 1.' (Claps the board for sound & camera sync) > CLAP !! < (The camera assistant dashes back off camera.)
There is a pause... all is quiet... then...
DIRECTOR: 'Action!' The actors play the scene.
DIRECTOR: 'Cut! Print!'
ASSISTANT DIRECTOR: 'Take us off the bell, please!' (The stage manager pushes a button and two single note electronic bell-buzzer tones can be heard throughout the stage. The flashing red lights stop. Doors can be opened and the crew can enter or exit the stage.)
SCRIPT SUPERVISOR: 'Printing 22B take 1.'
CAMERA OPERATOR: 'Checking the gate.' (He inspects the camera to make sure the film rolled correctly.)
CAMERA OPERATOR: 'Good for camera.'
ASSISTANT DIRECTOR: 'Moving on!'
2nd ASSISTANT DIRECTOR: 'That's school for Billy and Angela for 20 minutes!' (Ange and I are shuffled off the stage and into the school trailer outside where we must shift our brains from acting to education for 20 minutes until they call us back to the set for a rehearsal for the next scene.)

... And that's the way it was."
BILL

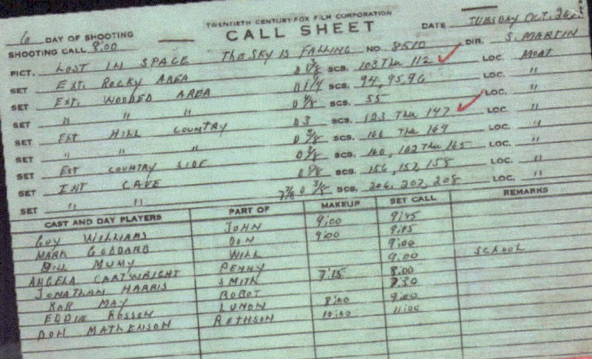

FYi A rare glimpse of some call sheets that were attached to a few of Bill's scripts.

LOST IN MEMORIES

"The huge hand-painted canvas skyline backdrop that was draped around our sand-filled campsite set on Stage 11 was truly a work of art. I wonder what became of it? So many props and sets were simply destroyed when productions ended on projects of the past. I see this image but I also see beyond its framing. I see the scaffolding above with the huge lights where the crew was perched making tiny adjustments for every shot. I see behind the backdrop, where it was always dark and the floor was filled with huge cables that you could trip over if you weren't aware of them. I see behind the camera where dozens of people were gathered constantly doing their specific jobs such as pulling focus on the camera and pushing the crane that held the camera and the camera operator forward or pulling it backward or side to side. I see the sound mixer sitting on his folding stool with headphones on listening to the scene as it was filmed, checking for unwanted outside noise that would force us to go 'back to one' and do it again. I see the sound assistant holding the boom mic up high and tilting it towards

whoever was speaking at the moment, being careful not to let the mic drop into the frame. I see the director sitting in his chair, higher than the other chairs, hoping this take would be a 'print.' I see the wardrobe and makeup and prop and special effects crew members sitting and standing. I see a few guys playing cards back by the huge closed door to the stage behind the gargantuan Ritter fan that loomed in front of the craft service corner near one of two heavy small doors that led in and out of Stage 11, one to a parking area and one into a foyer with a cigarette machine and a candy machine and a water fountain and the men's and women's bathrooms. I see the bright red lights above the doors illuminated, meaning we were filming and no one was to enter or exit the stage until the lights were extinguished. I see our parents sitting in our chairs, knitting and looking up once in awhile. I see our schoolteacher/welfare worker watching to make sure we weren't too close to whatever was about to explode. But mostly I just see a place I loved."
BILL

On The Set

"Our crew was hard-working and terrific. We would crank out an hour episode in eight days in what was scheduled for an unrealistic seven. Funny, Irwin is actually talking to June and Guy in this photo as he usually preferred to use his megaphone even if you were only a foot away."
ANGELA

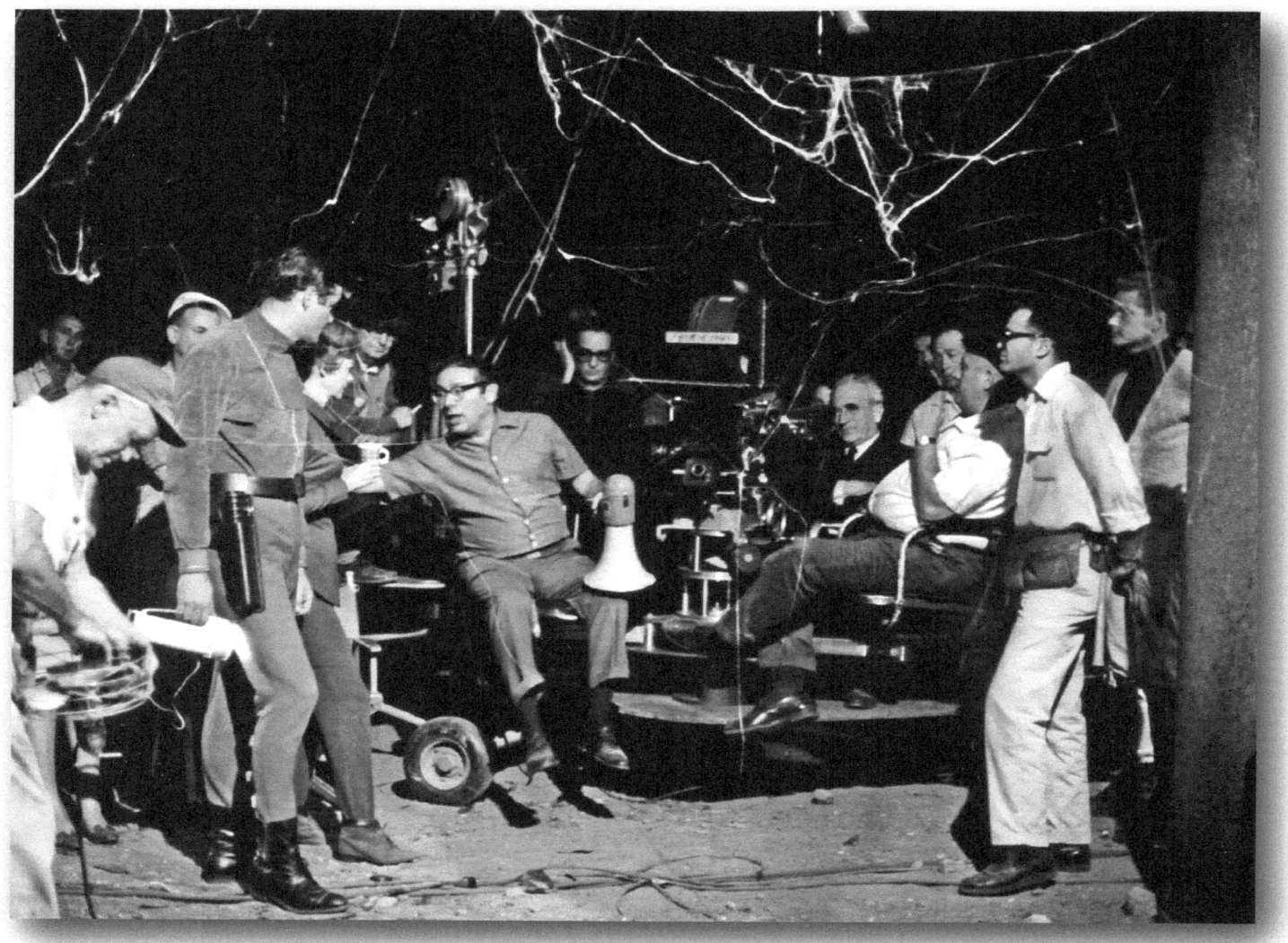

"The weekly Nielsen ratings would be tacked up by the craft service station, and we'd all be anxious to see how we did. We did real good. Between 30 and 40 million people watched Lost in Space every week!"
BILL

"We grew up in a unique world that had its own language... 'We're on a bell! Kill the fans. We had a boom shadow. Put a baby on the junior. Checking the gate. Raking 7. Single. Single. Tight Two. Take two steps camera left... the other way. This is M O S! Martini shot. Tits and lips.'... makes perfect sense to us."

FYI *Lost In Space* was filmed on two soundstages and in Season 1 on the backlot of 20th Century Fox studios. Now that backlot is Century City.
STAGE 5: 210' X 133' 40' high 28,274 square feet   STAGE 11: 130' X 125' 40' high 16,250 square feet

"The space race was on... could a family exist on an alien planet? What would daily life be like in the future? How would your clothes be washed, food be served, data gathered? When you think of it that way, you truly realize how imaginative *Lost In Space* was."
ANGELA

"Set designers tried to imagine what window coverings in the chariot would look like in the future. The best they could come up with was a heavy silver black-out tie-back café curtain. Today they would be high definition digital screens, but at the time, that probably seemed unimaginable."
ANGELA

"Irwin loved high tech props. 'This is called a flashlight, Billy.'"
BILL

"Our skyline backdrop was a great piece of artwork. Here you can see the catwalk above the set on Stage 11 where the camera crew adjusted the lights. It's also a nice color shot of our Season 1 wardrobe."
Bill

"Oh look... 'little mechanical men!' We laughed for years about that line. Out of this episode, the desk-sized version of the Robot was born."
ANGELA

"Director Don Richardson. He was a bad man. He was a very bad man. So I sent him to the cornfield."
BILL

"A bird's-eye view of the chariot taken during the pilot. Looks like 'danger, danger' in the form of some rubber rocks about to rain down on the Robinsons and Major West."
BILL

"Between takes we built puzzles and played word games like Scrabble. Marta always got mad when I challenged her words, but hey... they weren't real words."
BILL

"Even though the schedule may be tight with a certain number of pages to get done, there was always downtime. When not in school we would spend time playing games, hanging with the crew, or visiting the catering guy who we all nicknamed Hot Pot. Good food, hot coffee, water, and snacks are very important. A hungry crew makes for a grumpy set."
ANGELA

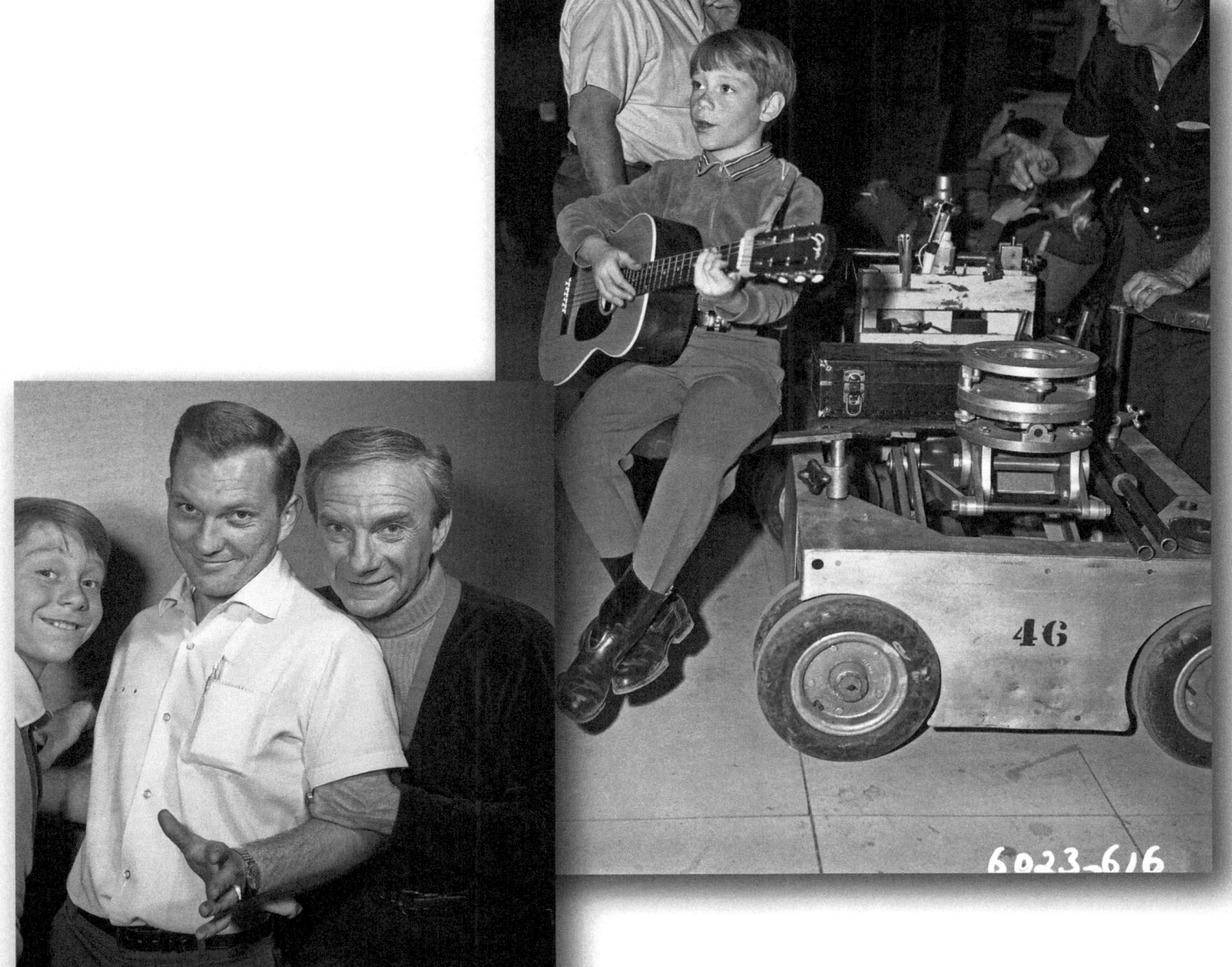

"Mike 'Hot Pot' was our craft service man. Coffee and donuts daily. Everyone liked him, he kept us all properly fueled. I made Hot Pot a villain in my *Captain Panther and Fox* comic book."
BILL

"During the years of production, I don't recall any of the cast going through any truly major life-changing drama at home, although Marta had some hard times in her marriage. But after the series ended, so did June's marriage, Mark's marriage, Marta's marriage, and eventually Guy's as well. Only Jonathan and Gertrude Harris and Bobby and Judy May made it through to the end. As of this writing, Ange has been married 45 years to her husband Steve and my wife Eileen and I have been together 35 years."
BILL

"Everyone in the cast smoked cigarettes, except Jonathan and June. Ange and I started smoking pretty soon after the series ended, too. We used to hide cigarettes in the bathrooms upstairs in the Old Writers' Building where we went to school and sneak up there and have smoke breaks. I imagine Frances Klampt knew... but we didn't think she did at the time. Ange smoked Virginia Slims menthols. I smoked Marlboros. We're all nonsmokers now."
BILL

LADIES ON DECK

"Take note: this is how space gals stand on the top deck while waiting for their space men to return."
ANGELA

Ready on the Set... Action!

FYI This is Bill's script schedule from January 8, 1965 - the third day of filming the pilot.

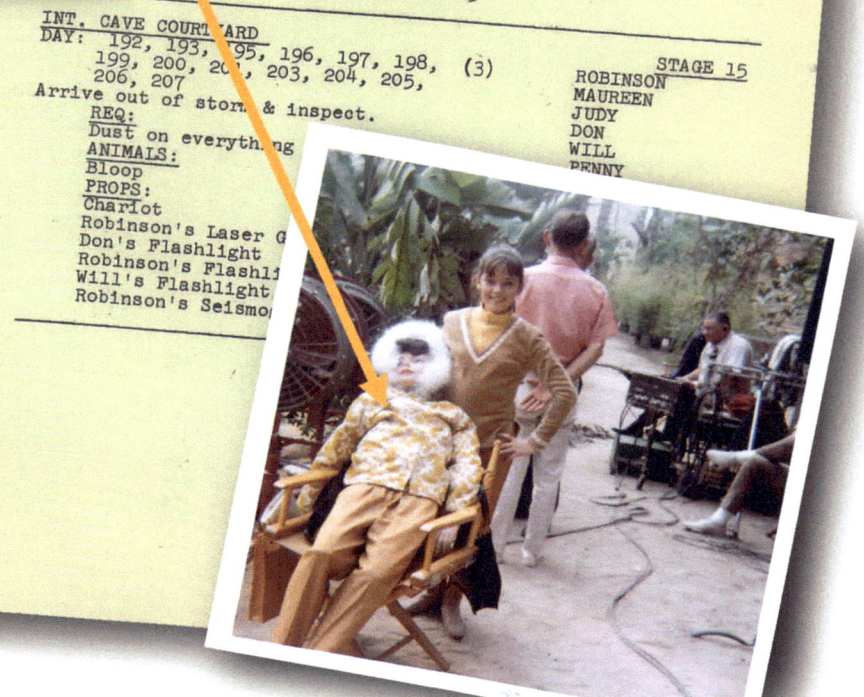

"Hey Dummy, that's my chair!"
ANGELA

Angela Cartwright Collection

"The jet pack sounded like a great idea, but since it wasn't a reality yet, our jet pack was us sitting on a boom and being raised into the air. Kind of like sitting on a seesaw all day. Kudos to Debbie for being such a good sport."
ANGELA

Guy's stunt double.

"The old 20th Century Fox lot was like a micro-city. There was literally everything you might want from a full-service commissary to the quaint micro-infirmary. A post office, a bank, and a dry cleaner were available for everyone's convenience. The Old Writers' Building hummed with the consistent sound of typewriter keys working on episodes and movie treatments. It was perched atop the permanent schoolhouse that was filled with books and old wooden school desks with names like Elizabeth Taylor and Roddy McDowall scratched into the surface. In the Executive Building there was a pool and sauna in the basement, a masseuse was ready and waiting for impromptu stress release. The old-time barbershop pole spun all hours with a shoe shiner always on call. A fully equipped salon held a plethora of wigs and mustaches, and manicurists who were always ready. The women's and men's wardrobe buildings had thousands of costumes from every era complete with hats, gloves, and shoes. The sound of multiple sewing machines filled the air when you entered. Talented people worked in every department exercising their skills daily.

The transportation of choice was golf carts that twisted and turned between the stages with script rewrites or urgent messages. Bicycles were seen whizzing back and forth and people were walking, always walking to get from one point on the lot to the other.

From the art department where the artist put pen to paper, to the Old Mill where sets were being built, this was this buzzing city of creativity that was the backdrop of my youth."
ANGELA

FYI 20th Century Fox was founded on May 31, 1935. Almost 84 years later, on March 20, 2019 it was officially acquired by Disney for $71.3 billion. 4,000 Fox employees lost their jobs as the merger became a reality.

"Love these never-before-seen pics behind the scenes. The episode was *The Oasis*, and was shot on the 20th Century Fox lot in front of the Executive Building. The camera shoots up to give the illusion of a giant Smith against the backdrop of the sky. A few episodes were shot on the 20th Century Fox backlot, but filming on the main studio lot was rarely done."
ANGELA

Holding On

"Here's something absolutely no one's ever known before... and I hesitate to share it now, because it holds the potential for distracting and changing the perception of my work in some of the very best *Lost in Space* episodes. But... when we first started filming the series, for awhile I didn't really know what to do with my hands when standing around in a scene of any length. Although my 'on planet' wardrobe had pockets, they were zipped closed and we couldn't put our hands inside them. So, I started resting my left hand on my belt. I did that a lot starting around episode six. I saw the shows when they ran on television for the first time like everyone else and when I did, I realized that I was doing that 'hand on the belt' thing way too much. I made a conscious choice to cut way back on doing it. But if you watch for it, you will now notice it and perhaps it will take you out of the drama that's in a few of those early great shows and change your perception a bit. Or... perhaps not."
BILL

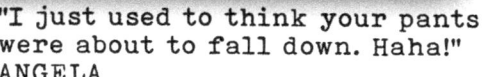

"I just used to think your pants were about to fall down. Haha!"
ANGELA

ANOTHER ONE BITES THE DUST

"There were many dust storm effects on the show but the one that stands out to me is the cosmic storm when Mr. Nobody gets upset near the end of the episode. Huge six foot Ritter fans with enormous wooden propeller blades were turned on and grit, dirt, and dust was projected into my face. Throw enough dirt and some will stick. I chewed on that grit for days. Showbiz is a dirty job, but someone has to do it."
ANGELA

A Script in the Hand...

FYI A page from Bill's original shooting script from Episode 2, *The Derelict*.

"This was taken on Stage 11, shot during the filming of *The Reluctant Stowaway*, July 1965. This was never approved for official release because Jonathan's face was partially in shadow."
BILL

Space Sounds of Music

"I brought my guitar everyday when we shot the pilot. And brought it often in summer when we shot the series. My first guitar was a nylon strung classical Goya. By Season 3 I'd traded it for a 1965 Gibson B-25N."
BILL

"I started playing the guitar just a few months before we shot the pilot. Irwin saw me playing in between setups of the exterior Jupiter 2 campsite sequence and he thought it would be a nice thing to add to the campsite scene. It was a very spontaneous decision on his part. I remember him asking me what songs I knew how to play. I named a bunch of tunes I knew from the Kingston Trio catalog as well as several traditional folk songs. As soon as I mentioned knowing how to play and sing *Greensleeves*, Irwin said, 'That's the one. Do that.' I later learned that it was because the song was in the public domain and he wouldn't have to pay to license it from a publisher. I must admit, that I still cringe when I hear my 10 year old self singing this, but I always enjoyed the opportunity to play guitar on the series."
BILL

Space Fun!

"The props that were created for the pilot and first season all looked great. But, unfortunately, they weren't all practical. The laser pistols were especially fragile. They were wired with a battery and lit up when you squeezed the trigger, which was very cool, but those wires were always shorting out and either not illuminating when you wanted them to, or they wouldn't shut off once turned on. The site and the circular piece on the end of the barrel of the guns were constantly breaking off, which resulted in a loss of shooting time while the prop men struggled with glue and tape and wires to repair them.
In Season 2, we were given silver streamlined laser pistols and rifles that were basically indestructible. But they didn't look anywhere nearly as cool as the original ones did."
BILL

FYI The laser guns weren't real!

FYI During filming of the Season 3 episode, *Condemned Of Space*, they built a lightweight stunt robot out of fiberglass, Styrofoam, and wood. No one was inside it for this scene, it was manipulated like a large puppet. A stuntman was doubling for Guy whose close-ups were added in later.

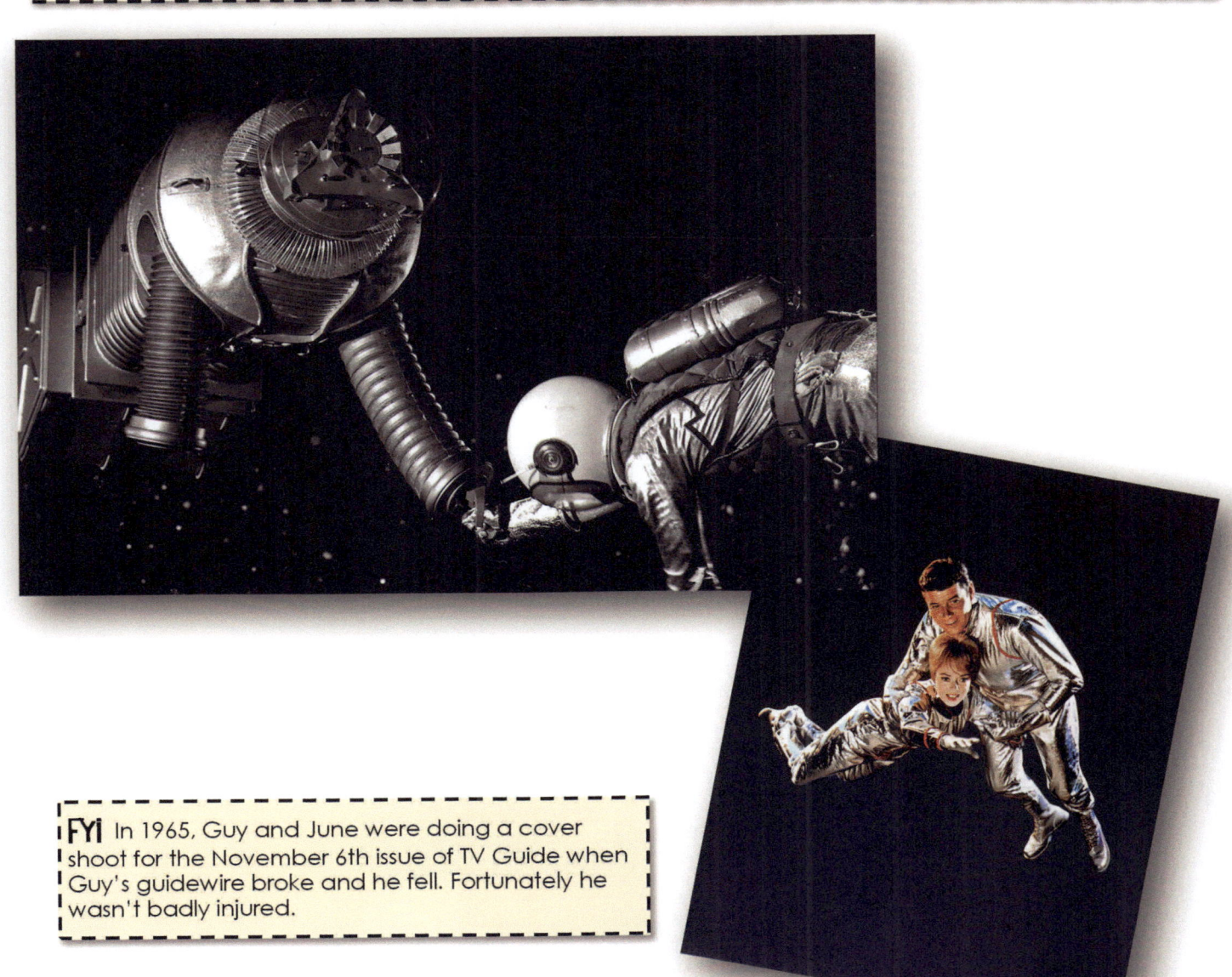

FYI In 1965, Guy and June were doing a cover shoot for the November 6th issue of TV Guide when Guy's guidewire broke and he fell. Fortunately he wasn't badly injured.

Troublemakers in Space

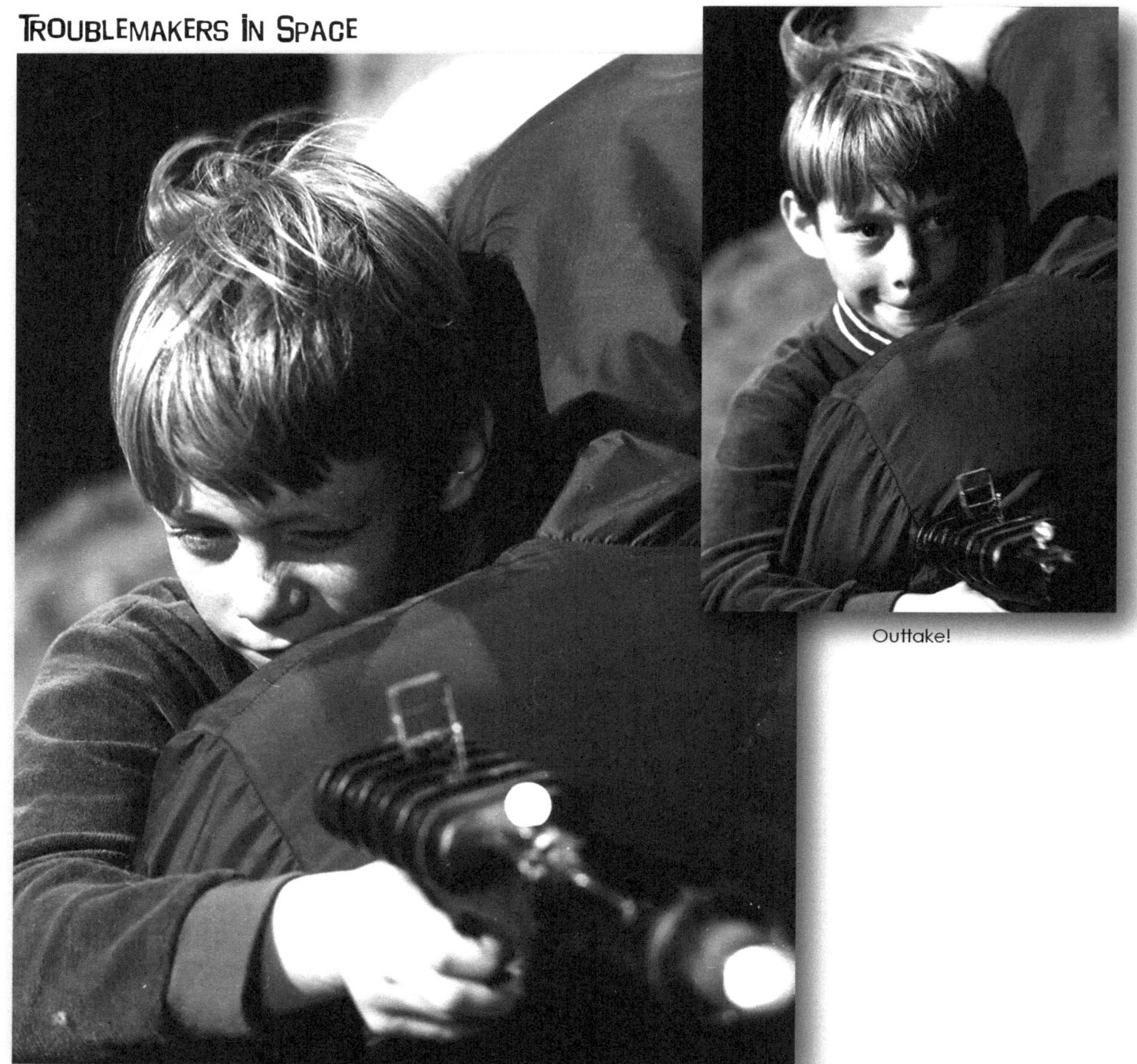

Outtake!

"There was one time, quite early into the series, when we got in trouble. It was August 1965. I was 11 and Ange was 12. It was really hot that day and we'd been filming under the lights in our heavy wardrobe for hours. We were on Stage 5. Before you open the double super heavy doors to enter the actual soundproof stage, there's a foyer to go through. At each end of it are restrooms, men's on the left, women's on the right. In the foyer itself there are candy and cigarette machines, big old theater ashtrays, and a trash can. Above the doors to each of the restrooms there are windows that crank open for ventilation.

It happened quickly and almost instantly escalated into full blown chaos... a water fight. One white paper cup of water tossed into a bathroom led to the foyer, the vending machines, both bathrooms, and especially Ange and me being totally drenched. And it was loud. She used to scream a lot.

Thinking about it right now, it seems like we should've been on the Disney lot instead of Fox, cuz it looked like something straight out of a Disney film. Two kids, who just happened to be starring in a TV show, yelling and tossing cups of water on each other and throwing them through the open windows into the bathrooms and battling it out like insane monkeys.

It was great.

Anyway, we actually got in trouble. They yelled at us. For real.

'People could slip and hurt themselves!'

'Look at your wardrobe!'

'Get yourselves into makeup right now!'

'There will be no more of this behavior! Is that understood?!'

So, we tucked our wet tails between our legs, grinned at each other, and picked up about 50 paper cups that we'd tossed.

I started it."

BILL

Family Scrapbook

"Colorized image from the pilot. Will's gonna break the rules soon and sneak out with a laser gun, shoot a giant cyclops, save Dad and Don's lives and get in trouble for doing it."
BILL

FAMILY TIES

Here's Looking At You, Kids

"After *The Sound of Music* filming ended, 20th Century Fox studios kept me on the lot and I completed my school year in the schoolroom in the Old Writers' Building.
This photo shoot was taken outside the gazebo on the town square set of *Peyton Place,* a popular prime time soap opera being filmed on the lot. I was cast in *Lost In Space* shortly before this photograph was taken. I am wearing the sailor dress I wore when I interviewed for the part of Brigitta von Trapp. It's a good thing I finally grew into my feet."
ANGELA

"This is a publicity picture from *Dear Brigitte*, a quirky 20th Century Fox feature film in which I co-starred with the great Jimmy Stewart. That movie earned me the title of 'first American actor to receive an onscreen kiss from Brigitte Bardot.' I went straight from *Dear Brigitte* into *Lost In Space*."
BILL

Laughs in Space

"We all had a real good time."
BILL

"You gotta laugh to keep your sanity."
ANGELA

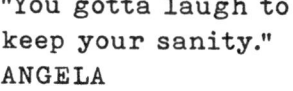

DOUBLE TROUBLE

"Mirror, mirror on the wall..."
ANGELA

"Who's the grooviest Penny of all?"
BILL

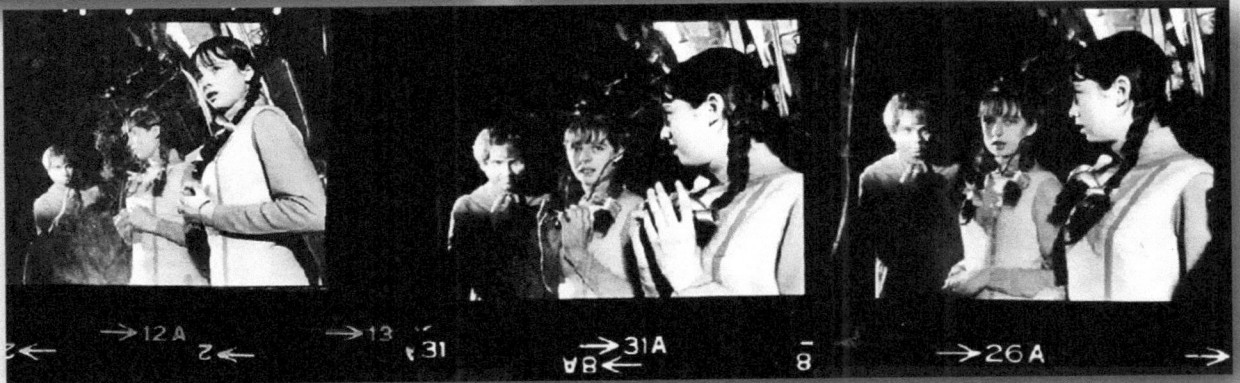

Flower Power

"I knew Penny was growing weed in the hydroponic garden, but THIS is freaky!"
BILL

"No Bill, I said WE were growing like weeds..."
ANGELA

That Time We Wore T-shirts!

"These solar panels above were very innovative and ahead of their time. Today they are called shade sails."
ANGELA

"I don't know why Judy, Penny, and Will are in t-shirts and Don, Maureen, and John are in parkas. Oh well, some like it hot I guess."
ANGELA

Baby, It's Cold Outside

"Oops the boom mic is in the shot."
BILL

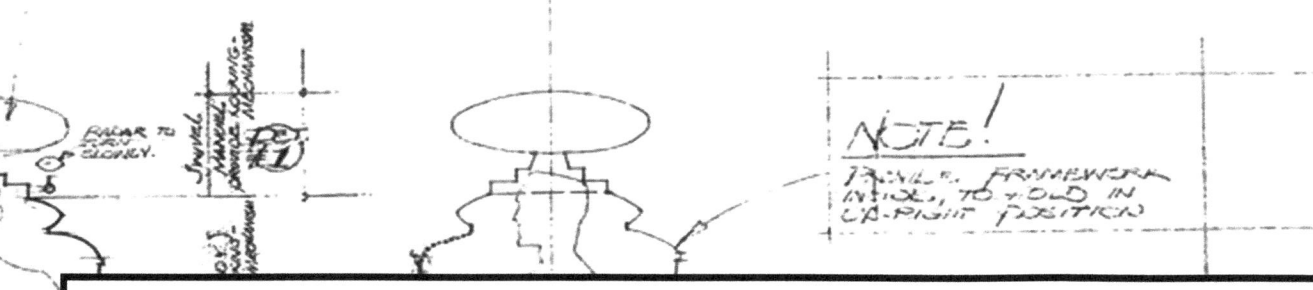

"I've told this story before, and so has Mark, but here's what really happened...

Once Bobby May was locked inside the robot, there was no way for him to get out on his own. One day, after Bobby had been particularly annoying during a long master scene on Stage 11, we were getting set to break for lunch. Our Special Effects Chief Stu Moody and his assistant Paul headed over to get Bobby out of the robot, but Mark and I intervened. We told them that we'd let Bobby out and they should just go to lunch.

So, everyone, crew, and cast evacuated Stage 11 and Mark and I stood by the open stage door looking at Bobby across the set, standing there in the sand next to a foam rubber rock and we decided we were gonna go to lunch too, and leave him stuck in there. I know. It was mean.

That's why after we'd left the stage and walked about 50 feet we both realized we couldn't go through with it and we turned around and headed back to free Bobby from being stuck inside that claustrophobic prop for the better part of an hour. As we entered the huge hangar-sized stage, we thought we would see the robot, right where we'd seen it a few minutes before of course. It was a good dozen yards away. But something was wrong. There was smoke coming out of the robot!

Now, you have to understand, the robot was a very complicated and dangerous prop. There were multiple batteries and cables and many different electrical systems in it. Mark and I started to run towards it. We were both scared. Had something shorted out? With Bobby trapped inside? Alone on Stage 11 at lunchtime when no one could hear him shout for help?!

It took a few seconds to reach him but it felt a lot longer. We got to Bobby and quickly unbolted the bubble top of the robot, fearing we'd find a charred smoldering corpse inside. That wasn't the case. Bobby was smoking a cigarette! Holding a small pen-flashlight in his right hand, his arm awkwardly bent up by his chin, he was reading the day's edition of *The Hollywood Reporter*! He was happy as a clam. He didn't even realize we had broken for lunch. 'Oh, hey, Mark, buddy. Hi Billy. Why are you guys here?' He didn't get the joke and Mark and I were relieved we hadn't killed him.

And that's the truth."

BILL

"Danger Will Robinson! We did this 'Smith uses Will as a shield' bit dozens of times. It was always pretty funny."
BILL

"The relationship between Will Robinson and Dr. Smith covered a lot of emotional ground. At times, it's a corrupted man manipulating an innocent child. At other times it's like the saying: 'child is father to the man.' Will was often straight man to Smith's eccentricity and greed, but he always, right from the very beginning, stood up to him and showed him the way to safety and redemption. In the end, after they grew to know each other well, I think they loved each other... and not in a creepy way!"
BILL

"Mark was always up for doing his own stunts. Or maybe he'd had a two-martini lunch."
BILL

FYI Paul Skelton, one of our special effects guys, was Red Skelton's brother. Red owned a piece of *Lost In Space*. It was well established in the 1950s and 1960s for the networks to give their big stars pieces of new television series to keep them happy.

"The head of our special effects crew was a man named Stu Moody. He looked sorta like Popeye. I believe we had more special effects on Lost in Space than any other show on television. Things were always exploding on our set. Jonathan was not comfortable being close to sparks, smoke, fire, and explosions. Any chance he got to have his double Handsome Harry do those shots instead of him he jumped at it. Jonathan had smart and generous advice regarding that subject that I have never forgotten. He used to say to me, 'Never deny a stunt person a check, Billy Person!' But, often they needed to be close on us with the camera as things went >BOOM< around us and Jonathan always needed reassurance that he was in no danger. He would call Stu Moody over and ask 'Well? Is it safe, Moody?' Stu would raise his right hand and give Jonathan the 'okey dokey' sign, meaning we were safe and ready to shoot. Jonathan would always groan in horror, because Stu had blown off three of his fingers! His 'okey dokey' sign was quite a sight to see."
BILL

1521-46

"Here's a super rare rehearsal shot from the first day of filming *The Great Vegetable Rebellion*, with Stanley Adams (out of wardrobe), Jonathan, and the llama. Jonathan asked one of our most prolific writers Peter Packer 'What on earth were you thinking?' Packer told him 'I didn't have another damn idea in my head.'"
ANGELA

"In 1997, TV Guide's *The 100 Greatest Episodes of All-Time* issue rated *The Great Vegetable Rebellion* as #76. Probably because it's so insanely bad it's unforgettable. The script called for the part of Willoughby to be a purple llama to play opposite Stanley Adams, who was a humanoid carrot. Willoughby the Llama was supposedly going to become a recurring cast member on the series. Well, Jonathan stood next to that llama for about three minutes before he refused to work with it. So they replaced the llama with character actor James Millhollin in a purple wig. I told that llama, 'It's a hard business, llama.'"
BILL

"I may be wrong... but I think Bill enjoyed his job."
ANGELA

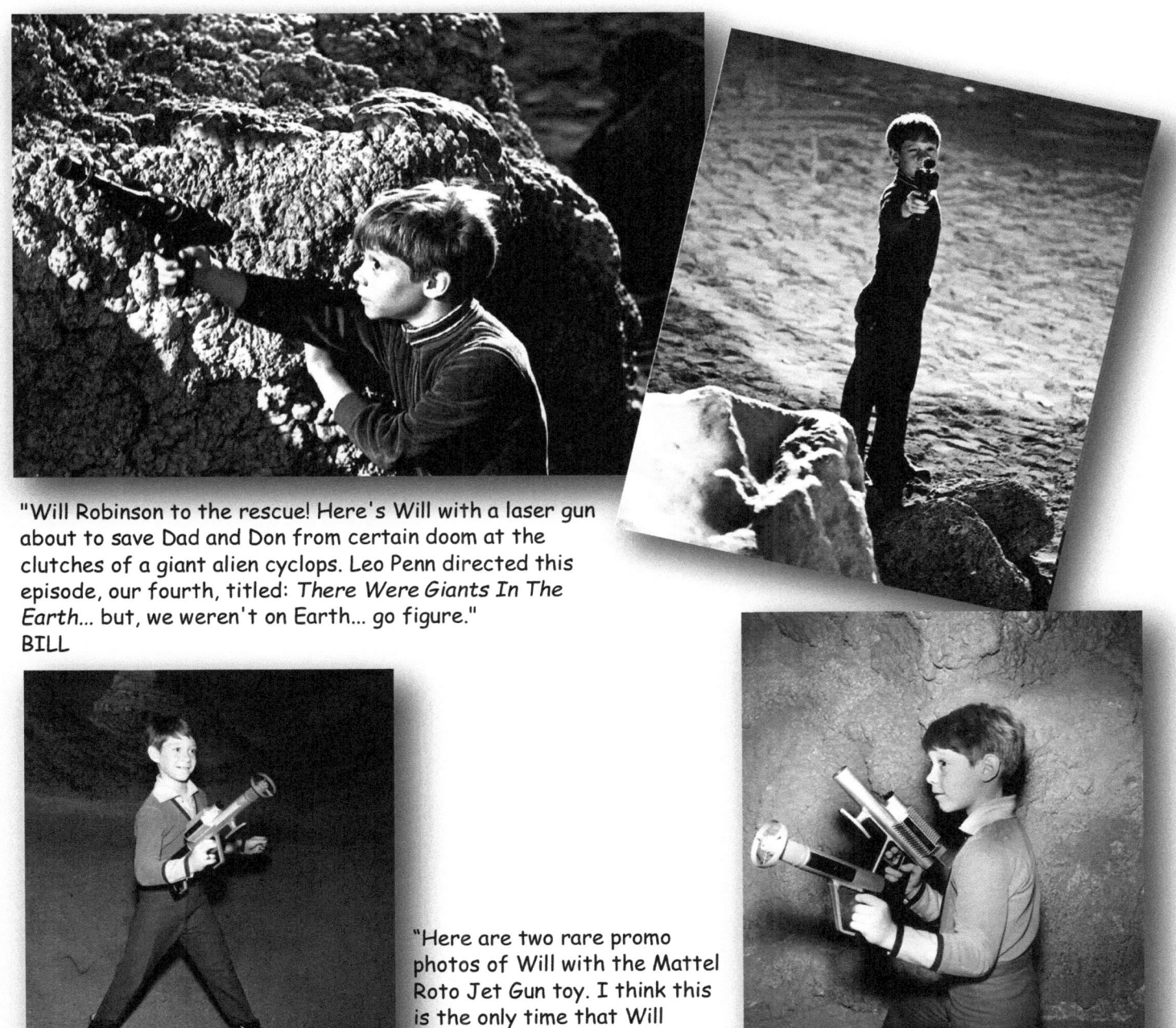

"Will Robinson to the rescue! Here's Will with a laser gun about to save Dad and Don from certain doom at the clutches of a giant alien cyclops. Leo Penn directed this episode, our fourth, titled: *There Were Giants In The Earth*... but, we weren't on Earth... go figure."
BILL

"Here are two rare promo photos of Will with the Mattel Roto Jet Gun toy. I think this is the only time that Will Robinson was seen on set with an actual licensed product."
BILL

"Who doesn't enjoy wearing a fur-trimmed parka during the dog days of summer in Los Angeles? These were not our favorite outfits and when the hoods with fur got wet they smelled like old stinky socks."
ANGELA

"Hmmm... Dad smells like an old pair of gym socks."
BILL

"One thing about Guy was how his chest felt like a stone slab. Every time he hugged me it was like being hugged by a brick wall. I remember thinking... wow... he's so strong. I guess it was the result of all those years of sword fighting."
ANGELA

Home, Sweet Home...

"Will was a master chess player. I never learned the game." BILL

Going Up?

"There was an upper deck and a lower deck inside the Jupiter 2. The upper deck was where the flight controls, astrogator, freezing tubes, weapons bay, etc. were located. The lower deck was where the living quarters, galley, laboratory, and flight seats were. The two decks were connected by a ladder and an elevator. The only problem was the upper deck was on Stage 11 and the lower deck was across the lot on Stage 5. So whenever we shot sequences involving the use of the elevator from the upper deck to the lower, the crew had excavated about five feet of space out of the stage floor. It was somewhat like being in a coffin getting lowered into the loam!"
BILL

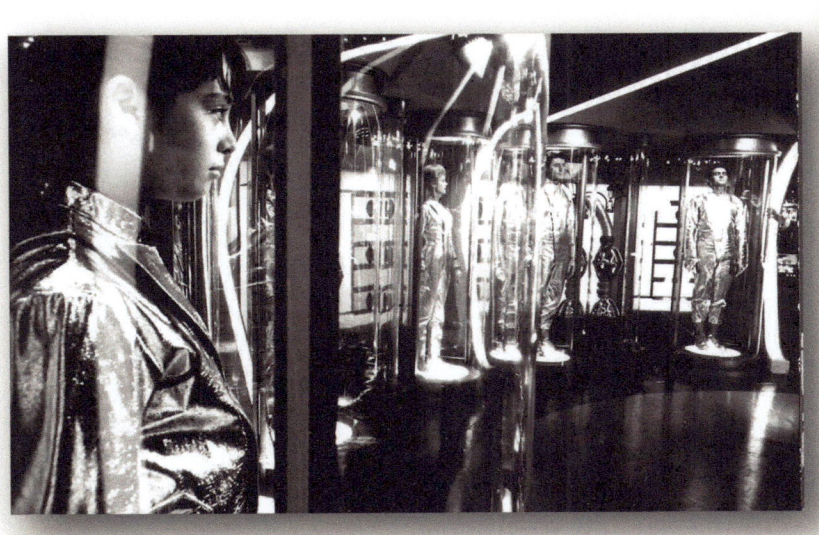

Down in the Basement

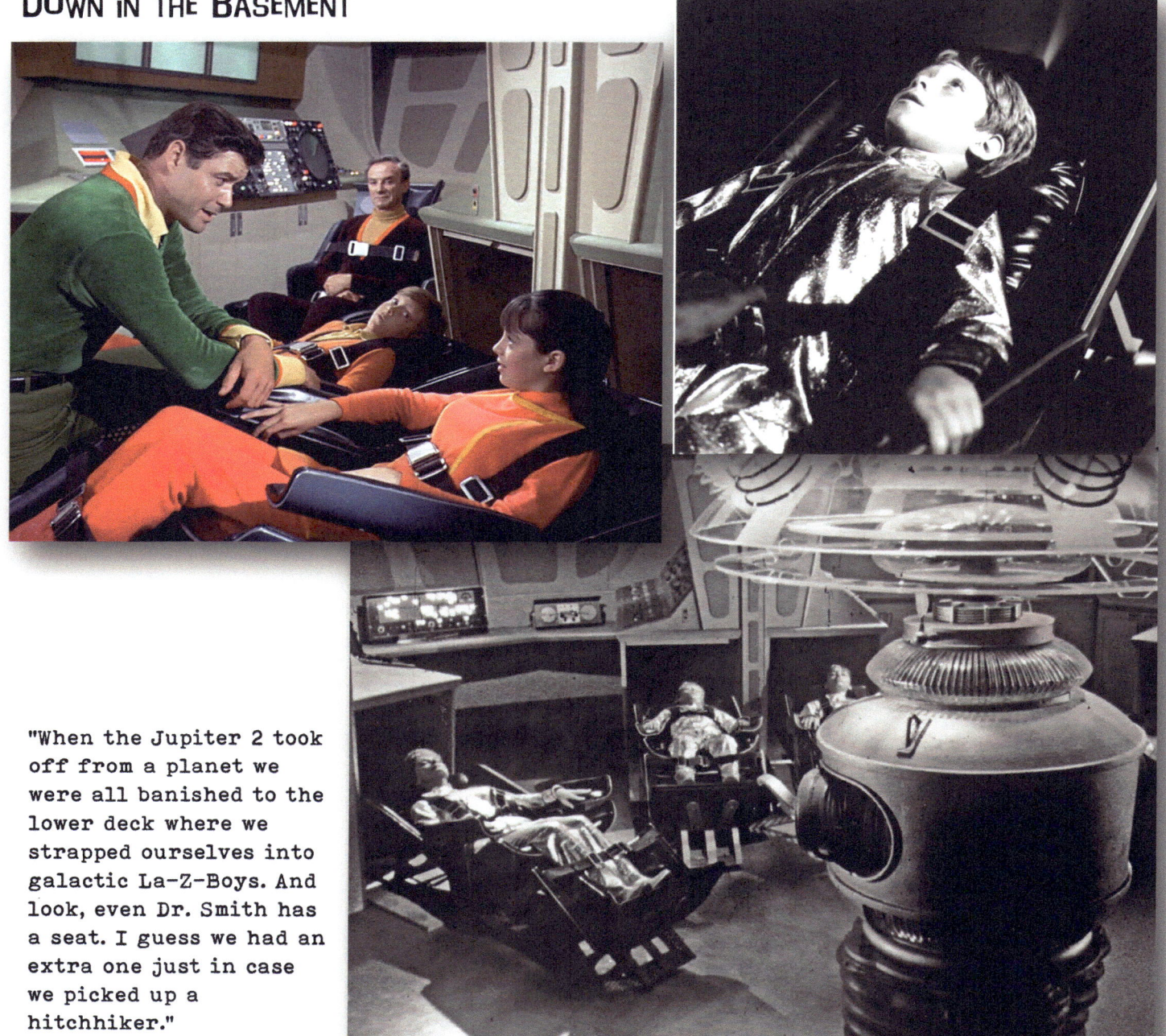

"When the Jupiter 2 took off from a planet we were all banished to the lower deck where we strapped ourselves into galactic La-Z-Boys. And look, even Dr. Smith has a seat. I guess we had an extra one just in case we picked up a hitchhiker."
ANGELA

The Happy Homemaker

"A few things I don't think we saw often enough were the washing machine that cleans, irons, and folds your clothes for you... our hydroponic garden filled with plenty of spacey greens... our fashionable pajamas and the cozy bedrooms on the bottom deck... and the fab hair dryer that styled your hair in an instant."
ANGELA

Below Deck

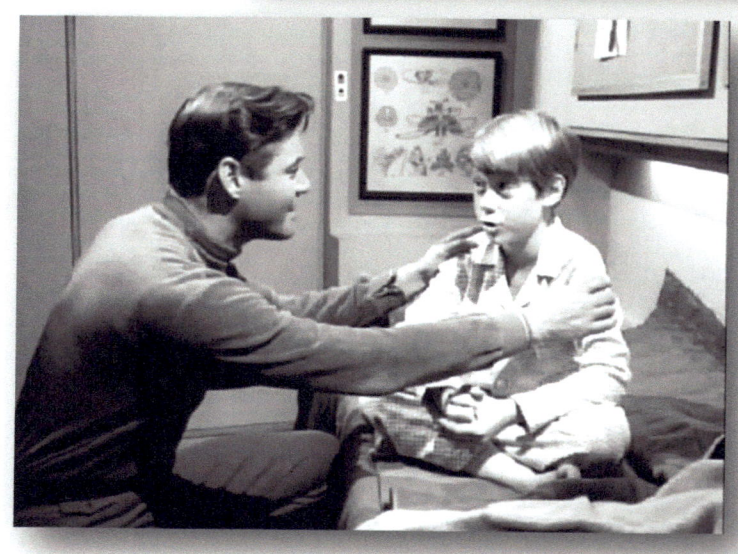

"Don't look behind the wall... it's our prop man placing food on the conveyor belt. Bill used to steal the candy from inside the jars on the wall you can see behind us. Heaven only knows how old that candy was or where it came from."
ANGELA

The Pajama Game

"Toothache or tinnitus? Here's a thought: who played the role of the dentist if needed?"
ANGELA

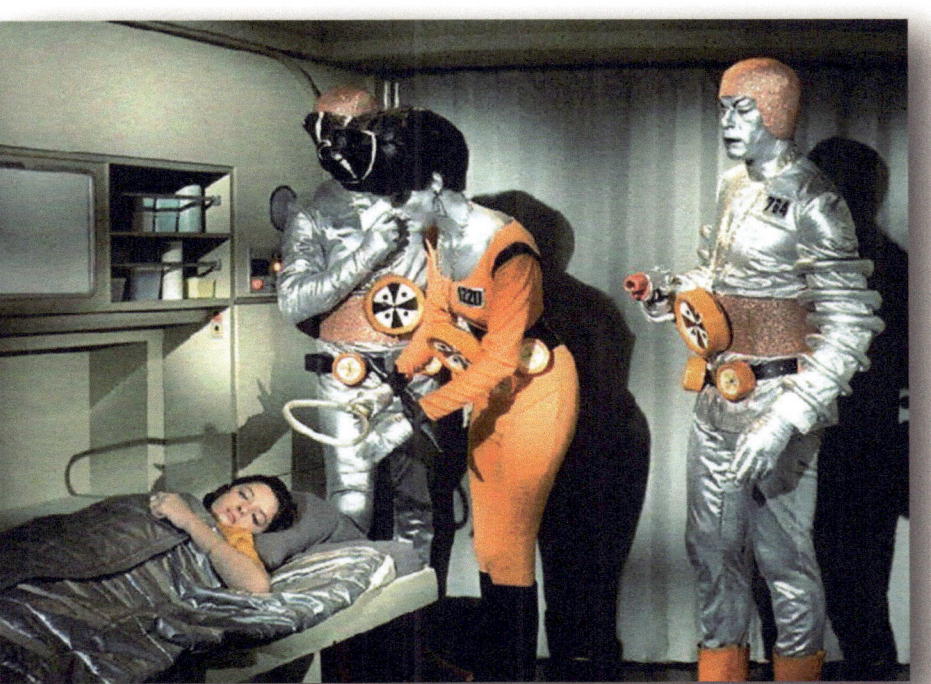

"Same two-shot, different seasons. We seem to stand like this a lot."
ANGELA

Space Gadgets

> **FYI** The Robinson women were great role models for girls growing up in the 1960s. Here Maureen, Penny, and Judy are taking charge of repairing the force field in the Season 3 episode *Hunter's Moon*.

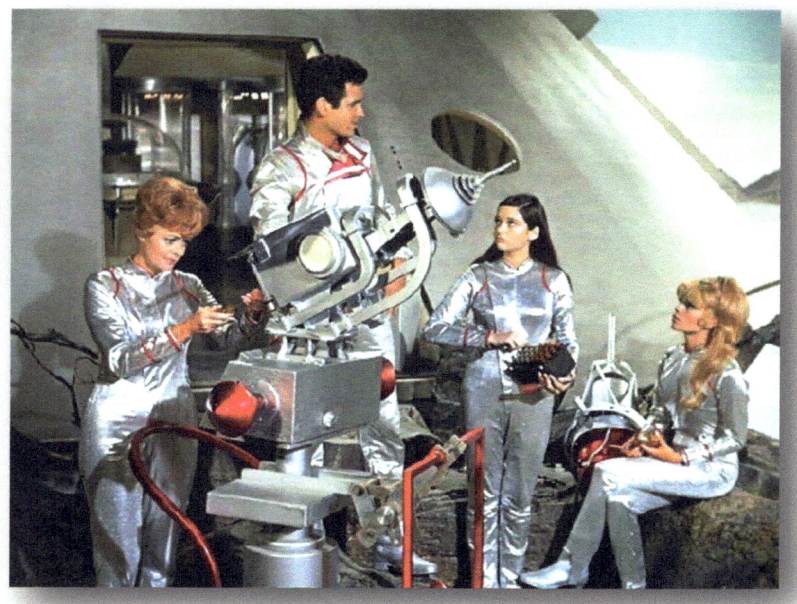

"Having a good laugh over our shenanigans that week. This was right before we were ordered to the top deck by John and Maureen so they could be alone."
ANGELA

"Will: 'You're a bad alien. You're a very bad alien!'
John: 'Send it to the cornfield, Son.'"
BILL

"Everyone loved it when Guy had the opportunity to add a little Zorro to Professor Robinson. Here he's 'laser fencing' with Michael Ansara. Now if he'd only had a cape!"
BILL

"Seriously, what is it about a guy who carries a big sword?"
ANGELA

"As Professor John Robinson, Guy brought a sense of power, wisdom, and trust to Lost In Space. When he starred as Zorro several years prior and he became an icon of pop culture, Guy was absolutely magnetic and dazzling. He came from a long lineage of fencers and he truly loved swordplay. I enjoyed watching him film scenes where the characters of Zorro and John Robinson melded into one. Guy had genuine fun when he was fencing on camera.

He was patient and generous with me and he taught me the basics of fencing during our years together on the series. I can hear him encouraging me in my memory, 'Six. Six. Court. Counter court. Head. Strike.' I can barely remember how to do it at all now (or if that even made sense) but I'll tell you this: learning how to fence from Zorro in a spacesuit was pretty cool!"
BILL

Bill Mumy Collection

"I really wanted to be Zorro!"
BILL

LET'S ROCK OUT TOGETHER...

"*The Promised Planet* is still one of the favorite shows to this day. We filmed the scene dancing to The Doors' *Twentieth Century Fox* (an odd coincidence). They redubbed it later with *Space-A-Delic* by jazz composer Pete Rogolo, which was written for the show. This scene was challenging. While Jonathan danced on the table, I had to rock out balancing on a soft cushion. Jonathan was a crack-up in that episode."
ANGELA

"My sisters are so hot they knock me off my feet."
BILL

"In the episode *One of Our Dogs is Missing*, this pup was with the Robinsons at the close of the show, but was curiously never seen again. He must have asked for too much money per episode.
Decades later, after Jonathan passed away, Marta adopted his dog named Zachary."
ANGELA

"A classic *Lost In Space* moment we have come to know and love."
ANGELA

"This photo is from the very first scene we ever shot featuring the trio of Smith, Robot, and Will... the seeds of what would come were already sprouting."
BILL

HELLO? AREN'T YOU STILL HERE?

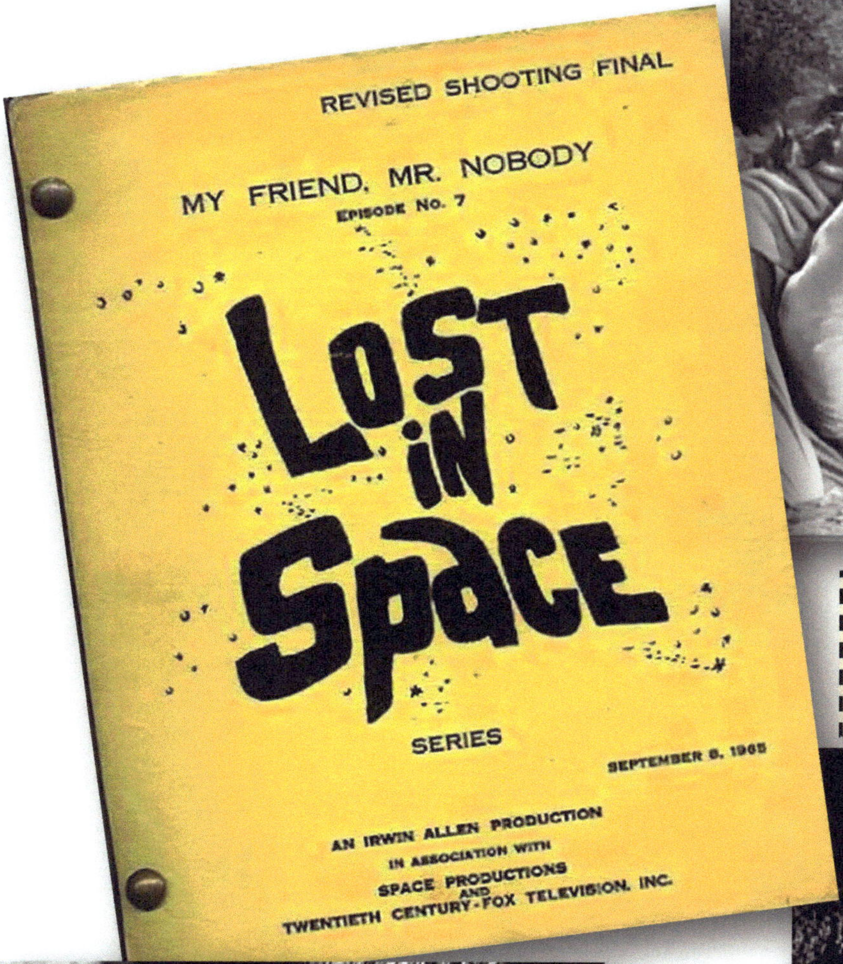
REVISED SHOOTING FINAL

MY FRIEND, MR. NOBODY

EPISODE No. 7

LOST IN SPACE

SERIES

SEPTEMBER 6, 1965

AN IRWIN ALLEN PRODUCTION

IN ASSOCIATION WITH

SPACE PRODUCTIONS

AND

TWENTIETH CENTURY-FOX TELEVISION, INC.

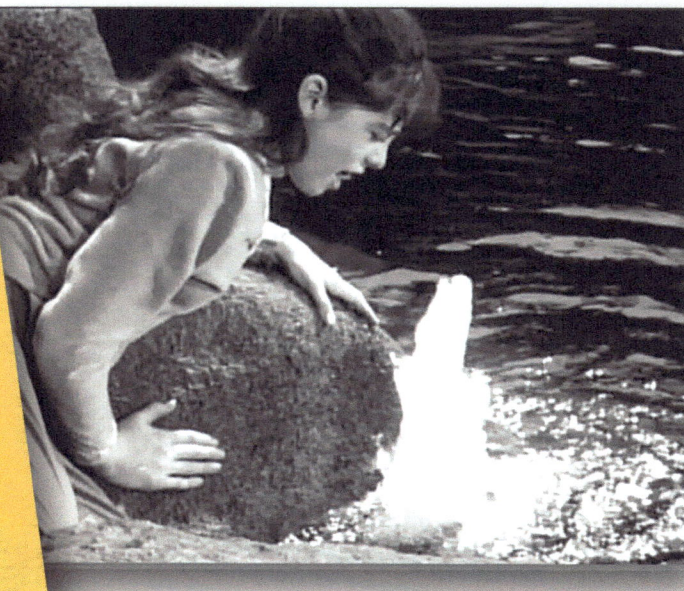

FYI William Bramley was the voice of Mr. Nobody. He was also the voice of Robby the Robot in the *Lost in Space* episode *War of the Robots.*

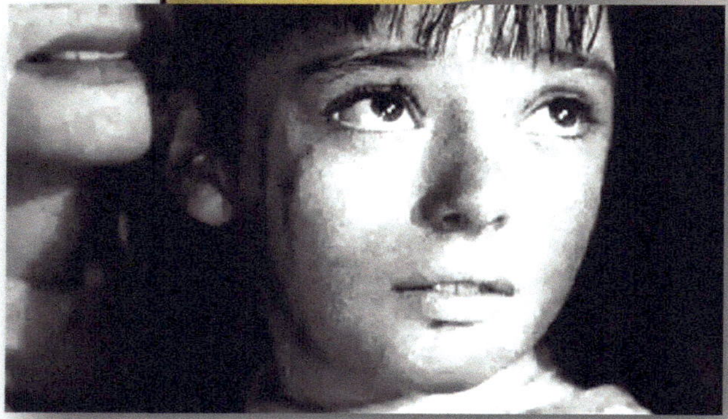

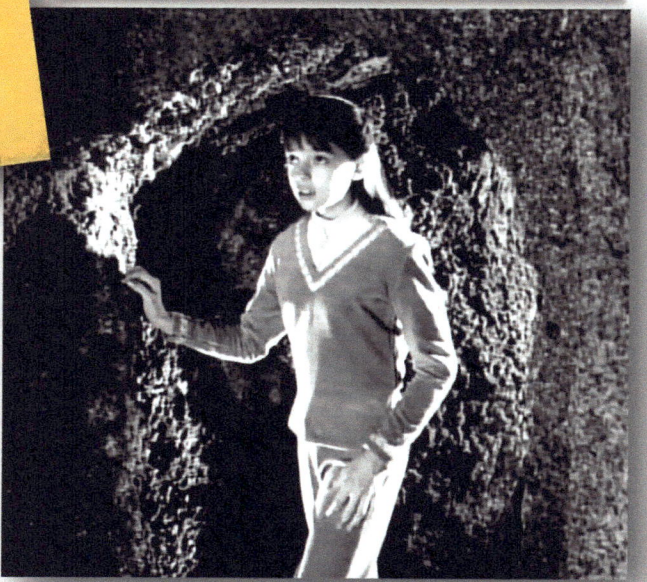

"*My Friend, Mr. Nobody* was my favorite episode. I loved the story, the ending, and the look of the show which was so dramatic in black and white. This episode was partly filmed on the backlot of the studio, where there was a mise en scène of plants, painted rocks, and a body of water. Later the voice of Mr. Nobody was dubbed in, but during filming, the script girl read the lines off camera as Penny scanned the cave walls for a glimpse of where the voice was coming from."
ANGELA

"A perfect example of how detailed our pre-production was. These Travel Action Maps were drawn for several episodes to show the relationship of the Jupiter 2 to where Mr. Nobody's cave was or where the drilling site was."
ANGELA

"I love this pic. It has a classic photographic noir look. We are all in the moment... looking at a cutout circle attached to a stick... pretending we are looking at the force that was Mr. Nobody."
ANGELA

Return from Outer Space

"It's difficult for me to choose a single favorite episode, but I think mine is *Return From Outer Space* for the simple fact that Will did make it back to Earth, and it was modern day (even though it looked like the 1940s when it was supposed to be the late 1990s). It was our first season Christmas episode, and Will was able to return to his family with a bottle of carbon tetrachloride and save the day. It still makes me angry that the people of Hatfield Corners, Vermont wouldn't let the poor kid make a phone call to Alpha Control."
BILL

FYI Reta Shaw played the role of Aunt Clara, she had been in *Mary Poppins* a year earlier. Sheila Mathews (Irwin Allen's wife) made her first of three appearances in *Return From Outer Space*. The episode aired December 29, 1965.

A Penny For Your Thoughts

It's Not Easy Being Green

"Don't make him angry, you wouldn't like him when he's angry."
ANGELA

The Second Time Around

FYI The release of *Lost (and Found) in Space 2 - Blast Off into the Expanded Edition* was chosen to commemorate the 55th anniversary of the first episode of Season 2, *Blast Off Into Space*, which premiered on September 14, 1966. The release of the original version of this book had been timed for the 50th anniversary of the series premiere.

"LOST IN SPACE" ORBITING IN COLOR -- The cast of producer Irwin Allen's exciting 20th Century-Fox TV series, "Lost in Space," is heading your way in color during its second season on the air, Wednesday, Sept. 14 over CBS-TV. Shown clockwise, from top to bottom, around the friendly robot, are: Jonathan Harris, Mark Goddard, Marta Kristen, Billy Mumy, Angela Cartwright, June Lockhart and Guy Williams.

LOST IN SPACE
CBS-TV-COLOR WEDNESDAY NIGHT

JONATHAN HARRIS
HAS PRAISE FOR
CHILD CO-STAR

Contrary to the traditional abhorrance of young thespians as usually expressed by adult actors, Jonathan Harris has no fear of child actors.

It is apparent in the way he plays Professor Zachary Smith to Billy Mumy's Will Robinson in Irwin Allen's production of "Lost in Space." The two are perfect foils in the 20th Century-Fox Television series.

"Billy is the delight of my life," raves Harris in his most resonant tones. "He is unlike any other child actor I have ever worked with.

"He has keen perception, an extensive knowledge of things ⬚able and things theatrical.

"Actually, television production is an unnatural world for children. They spend their days in an adult world to which they are not geared. They are often precocious and over extend themselves in a way that is unbecoming to a child and to an actor. But happily, Billy has been able to avoid these pitfalls.

"I feel there is a fine chemical reaction between the two of us that is good for us and the show. He is a very dear boy and believe me, it is a pleasure doing business with him.

"Lost in Space" is seen every Wednesday on ABC-TV.
W   #

LOST IN SPACE
CBS-TV-COLOR WEDNESDAY NIGHT

"LOST IN SPACE" -- FILLERS

There isn't much room in outer space for swashbuckling. But Guy Williams, noted for his gallantry with the sword, makes the best of it. If he can't subdue with his wits the villains on Irwin Allen's 20th Century-Fox Television series "Lost in Space," seen every Wednesday on CBS-TV, he resorts to computers. "I have no fear, they will save the day," says Williams.

***

Although June Lockhart may have every machine and device ⬚ible for doing housewifely chores in outer space on Irwin ⬚ ⬚ ⬚ ⬚ ⬚ ⬚ ⬚ ⬚ ⬚ion production of "Lost in

---

LOST IN SPACE
CBS-TV-COLOR WEDNESDAY NIGHT

MUMY AND HARRIS MAKE
SPACE-AGE TEAM ON ABC-TV

"He's great!" is young Billy Mumy's vocal reaction to working with Jonathan Harris in Irwin Allen's production of "Lost in Space." Harris echoes the same sentiment when talking about Billy.

Their respective roles of Dr. Zachary Smith and Will Robinson do not exactly represent a Damon and Pythias relationship, nor does it reflect the enmity between Dr. Frankenstein and his monster. Their regard for each other lies somewhere in between the two extremes.

"Smith really isn't such a bad guy," reasons Billy. "He's just some place in outer space where he doesn't want to be and he's trying desperately to get back to earth. He doesn't want to hurt anyone."

If Billy were lost in an earthly desert with a man like Smith, would he act the same way?

"Under the same circumstances, yes," he answers succinctly.

But what does Billy think about Jonathan Harris, Zachary Smith's alter ego?

"He's great! What else can I say except that he's great! Billy repeats with boyish enthusiasm.

"Lost in Space" starring Billy, Guy Williams, June Lockhart and Jonathan Harris with Angela Cartwright, Marta Kristen and Mark Goddard is produced by 20th Century-Fox Television and is seen every Wednesday over ABC-TV.
X   #

FYI The official 20th Century Fox Television press kit from 1967. This gem was found buried in a trunk of Angela's where it had been stored for more than half a century.
Notice the obvious typos on two of the pages referencing the show airing on ABC-TV!

Happy Birthday in Space!

"Pretty much everyone's birthdays were celebrated on the set. A piece of cake would be served to the entire cast and crew, and then we would all sing 'Happy Birthday.' It was always a positive and fun experience."
ANGELA

"I still have a couple of those spacemen from that cake. But you knew that, right?"
BILL

Bill Mumy Collection

SISTERLY LOVE...

"Not everyone knows that my sister is actress Veronica Cartwright. In 1964 she was cast as Jemima in the *Daniel Boone* series and was on that show for two years. It was a 20th Century Fox production but she was in a totally different location. I was shooting *Lost In Space* on the Pico Boulevard lot, and Veronica was on the 20th western lot in Hollywood on Western Avenue and Santa Monica Boulevard. Our paths didn't cross except at dinner every night at home.

The huge Fox studio backlot was first built in 1926 on a Culver City ranch in Los Angeles. Before much of it was sold off in the 1960s to become Century City, it was four times the size of its current 53 acres. When I heard of the Disney acquisition of 20th Century Fox, I must admit there was a pang in my heart. While Disney has acquired most of the Fox assets, Rupert Murdoch kept the historic studio lot where we filmed the interior scenes for *The Sound of Music* and shot *Lost In Space.* There were so many blockbusters filmed on that studio lot including *Hello Dolly, Butch Cassidy and the Sundance Kid, Planet of the Apes, Poseidon Adventure, Die Hard*, and the list goes on and on.

In May 1998 I was invited to the grand opening of Fox Studios Australia in Sydney. I was honored to introduce Shirley Jones' live performance with Hugh Jackman. The show was truly an amazing event with a star studded line-up. At the conclusion of the performances I glanced behind the curtain and saw Mr. Murdoch standing alone, looking up at the dazzling, sparkling display of fireworks that were exploding above us.

How I wished I had my camera with me for that photograph. As the old adage goes, 'a picture speaks a thousand words.'"

ANGELA

Angela's sister Veronica joining in at a party with the *Lost in Space* cast. (Right) Vintage teen magazine clip of the Cartwrights and the Mumys.

Robert Goulet's surrounded by Cartwright sisters: Angela (left) of Lost In Space & Veronica (once Daniel Boone's daughter).

Angela's TV brother-in-space, Billy Mumy, proudly presents his real, down-to-earth parents. Meet Mr. & Mrs. Charles Mumy!

Photos from Angela Cartwright Collection

Would This Face Lie?

"During the three years I worked on *Lost in Space*, I very rarely got sick, but it happened a few times. Once, I had a high fever and a really bad inflamed sore throat so my parents kept me home for a day of bed rest. Well, of course that messed up the shooting schedule a bit as some scenes had to be switched around or I had to be written out of something. Our production manager actually had the gall of coming to our house and going up to my bedroom to confirm that I was really under the weather. That pissed my mother off. Whatever, I got well quickly and the next night I went out to the Daisy Club in Beverly Hills with Cristina Ferrare."
BILL

Hanging Out on the Fox Lot

"Though rivals for ratings on the airwaves, *Batman* filmed on the 20th Century Fox lot on a stage near us. Here I am with Adam West sharing an interesting moment... a teenage girl and a man in a robe and tights."
ANGELA

"*The Green Hornet* was a short-lived favorite of mine. The tone of the series was very different from *Batman*, it was serious and done without much campy stuff. The masks that Van Williams and Bruce Lee wore as The Green Hornet and Kato were molded hard plastic and I thought they were the coolest things I'd ever seen. And the Black Beauty car was spooky and I dug sitting in that as often as I could. I never really got to know Van although he seemed like an easygoing guy, but I did become friendly with Bruce Lee back then. He was truly amazing. A unique, one of a kind, totally impressive talent. He was always very nice to me and he taught me a few martial arts kicks. Bruce and I did a personal appearance together for charity back in 1968 at Santa Monica City College (where I eventually attended) and I wish there were photographs of us from that, but I've never come across any. I consider myself very lucky to have spent some quality time with him. His son Brandon was a very close friend of mine. We shared a birthday and had some crazy adventures together. Both gone so young. Tragic losses."
BILL

Bill Mumy Collection

"Posing with Burt Ward outside Stages 10 & 11. You can see the open door to our school trailer in the background."
ANGELA

"Being a huge comic book geek I was pretty excited when *Batman* started filming. I remember Burt Ward coming over to our set to meet Ange and me the very first week they began production. I thought his wardrobe looked really good, but the flesh-colored tights seemed stupid to me. I guess they didn't want to show his hairy legs and he didn't want to shave them. I always thought Adam's cowl looked silly and to my eye he had noticeable perspiration stains under his armpits a lot. Adam was very nice and he was easy to talk to. Burt was nice for a few weeks and then he got a huge ego and was considered by most everyone on the Fox lot to be a huge pain. Years later, he changed his tune. Marta dated him for a brief time. What I enjoyed most was sitting in the Batmobile when it was parked nearby. I thought that was pretty cool."
BILL

Photos from Angela Cartwright Collection

"Once school hours were completed I would busy myself with art or reading (*Nancy Drew* was my favorite at the time), puzzles, or writing to my pen pals. I didn't get into too much trouble but sometimes Bill and I would steal away (when we knew they wouldn't need us on set for awhile) and explore other stages on the lot. Once on the deserted set of the movie *Fantastic Voyage* we climbed into the huge stomach and bounced around. When we were feeling especially brave we used to climb down the stairs to explore under the stages where there were huge fans in the antiquated cooling system. It was totally creepy, dark, and eerie. I was scared to death and I think Bill was too, but we used to explore it anyway. We would have gotten into tons of trouble if anyone had ever found out because I'm pretty sure it was dangerous down there. So I'm confessing now to get it off my chest."
ANGELA

"I clearly remember the day I discovered the underground labyrinth-like tunnels that run underneath the entire studio. There were two closed doors on the street between stages and one day I turned the doorknob and it opened. It led to a pitch black long concrete stairway. I found the light switch on the cement wall and turned it on and ventured down alone. Once at the bottom, I found another light switch and the entire tunnel was illuminated. You could feel the buzzing of power and see huge generators and fans. Venturing into one of the tunnels, it got very hot and spooky. I went and got Ange and convinced her to check it out with me. She was recalcitrant and scared, but it filled us with adrenaline. It was kinda sexy in a way. We explored those tunnels several times. It was like the Robinsons exploring ruins of alien civilizations."
BILL

"Eating lunch at the Fox commissary was surreal. You'd see Batman, the Green Hornet and Kato, folks from *Peyton Place* eating with folks from *Lost in Space*, aliens and cowboys, legendary movie stars, and the crew of the Seaview submarine, all in wardrobe and makeup queuing up for a good table. Everyone chatting and hanging out together. I always liked the commissary's clam chowder, while Mark enjoyed champagne."
BILL

QUEEN AND KING OF FRECKLES...It's lovely Patricia Morrow of the thrice-weekly ABC-TV series, "Peyton Place," matching her "sun etchings" with 10-year-old Billy Mumy, one of the stars of the CBS-TV adventure series, "Lost In Space." Billy won the contest by a nose-full of freckles.

"Back in the 1960s when we were filming the series, the 20th Century Fox lot was a really busy and wonderful place to be. Production was at peak capacity. Feature films like *Hello Dolly*, *Fantastic Voyage*, *Planet of the Apes*, and *Valley of the Dolls* were filming next to weekly TV series like *Voyage to the Bottom of the Sea*, *Batman*, *Green Hornet*, *Peyton Place*, *12 O'Clock High*, *Time Tunnel*, *Daniel Boone*, *Julia*, and others. I had worked prolifically at all the major studios before being under contract for *Lost in Space*, so I kinda knew many of the actors who were cast in these various projects. I'd estimate that Ange and I went to lunch together along with our mothers about 65 percent of the time. The rest of the time I'd either go off lot with Mark in his dark blue Fiat convertible to Duke's restaurant or I'd go to the fabulous Fox commissary and join some of the actors I'd worked with in the past, while my mother went and visited friends whom she'd worked with on the lot back in the 1940s when she was a writer's assistant.

My agent, Howard Rubin, also represented Ryan O'Neal, who was starring in *Peyton Place*, so I knew Ryan pretty well. I'd worked with Barbara Parkins years prior on a Universal TV pilot starring George Gobel called *My Uncle Elroy*, so I became quite friendly with the *Peyton Place* cast: Barbara, Ryan, Mia Farrow, Patricia Morrow, and Chris Connelly. I'd eat with them often and for awhile, Mia Farrow would have me sit next to her and she'd call me her 'boyfriend.' Those were fun lunches. Once she started dating Frank Sinatra though, Mia's vibe changed in a dramatic way and nobody really goofed around with her anymore."
BILL

FYI The Fox commissary still features the original Art Deco statues, vintage lighting fixtures, and star-studded murals from when it was originally called the Café de Paris. The murals were painted by Haldane Douglas, who would later receive an Oscar nomination for Art Direction on *For Whom the Bell Tolls*. While not open to the public, the commissary has been featured in many Fox films and television series.

Angela Cartwright Collection

"My mom went to the set with me everyday. She would knit, read, and answer every piece of fan mail I received. It's a commitment being the parent of a child in show business, for there always needs to be a parent or guardian on the set at all times. I could always count on my mom, she was always there for me. My sister Veronica was working as Jemima in *Daniel Boone* and my mom's sister Mary used to be her guardian and go to the set with her as my dad was working full-time."
ANGELA

"We often went to lunch together with our moms, Margaret and Muriel. They were very different personalities, but they got along fairly well. We'd leave the studio sometimes and go to Century City and eat at the Broadway department store. Many times we went wearing our space wardrobe! No one ever hassled us, even once. Angela would buy a *Nancy Drew* book or a British Invasion record, and I'd buy a *Hardy Boys* book or a folk album."
BILL

Bill (in his 'Will Becomes Smith' makeup) gets a hand from his mother Muriel as he enjoys his clam chowder in the commissary.

Angela Cartwright Collection

"My stand-in was Ann Merman (above right). She was always nice to me, but she sprayed her hair with so much hairspray it was incredibly stiff and never moved an inch. I always marveled at that and thought how uncomfortable that must have been when she slept. Or maybe she just removed the whole thing and placed it on her nightstand at night."
ANGELA

"Sandy Gimpel became my stand-in for Seasons 2 and 3. By the middle of Season 3, I caught up to her in height. Sandy has enjoyed a long career as a stunt woman and has appeared in that other space show *Star Trek*."
BILL

Bill and Sandy Gimpel reunited.

Bill Mumy Collection

The Driving Forces

Bill Mumy Collection

"Guy drove a red Maserati convertible. June drove a Lincoln, and on occasion, a vintage fire truck! Mark had a dark blue Fiat convertible. I loved riding shotgun in that car with Mark! Marta had a Volvo. Jonathan a blue Cadillac. Ange arrived in a white Chevy. My mom drove a metallic brown Jaguar Mark II. Gorgeous car. Every night when we wrapped, she'd toss me the keys and I'd drive that Jag all around the Fox lot for about 10 minutes all by myself. I very much enjoyed that ritual and I still drive a Jag."
BILL

"I never really noticed what cars the cast were driving into work everyday. I do remember Irwin Allen driving a Rolls Royce. After the show ended I would drive my Camaro to school on the lot every day. I was never really into cars, the way Bill is. I must say that my Camaro and the 8-track in it was kinda cool. Irwin's old Rolls was subsequently owned and driven by Kevin Burns."
ANGELA

Kevin Burns driving Irwin Allen's Rolls Royce. Note the license plate: 1 IA.'

"Lou Schumacher, who was the animal trainer, young Debbie, and 10 year old me. My mom took this photo outside of Stage 11 when we shot the pilot."
BILL

Photos from Bill Mumy Collection

"My mom took this photo of Mark and I while we were shooting the pilot in January 1965. My mom loved Mark. She called him 'my other son'... and said the same thing to him that she often said to me, 'Mark, I love you, but you're a fool.' My mother was an interesting woman."
BILL

"I knew every single inch of the Fox lot like the back of my hand back in the day. I knew exactly which candy machines had Zagnut candy bars stocked in them and which doors were always locked. I knew how to get up to the roofs and how to get down into the underground tunnels that were used as bomb shelters during WWII because the military wouldn't let the studios camouflage the huge soundstages, so they somewhat served as decoys for airplane hangars (which were indeed camouflaged) in case the Japanese tried to bomb hangars. I knew exactly where Teddy and 'The Roach Coach' food truck would be at any given time. I knew who was shooting what and where and when it would be cool to check out certain closed sets. I knew who was a jerk and who was nice and above all else, I always... always knew my lines."
BILL

FYI There are plaques on each of the soundstages on the Fox lot commemorating key films and television series filmed there. This is the plaque from Stage 5.

Photo by Tom McLaren

"I loved the 20th Century Fox lot. And my mom did too. She had worked on the lot as a writer's secretary for 11 years before she married my father. So, she had quite a few friends who still worked there. My mom would wander around and visit with her old pals once in awhile."
BILL

Angela Cartwrright Collection

"A first generation hippie. Going to school on the lot in 1969."
BILL

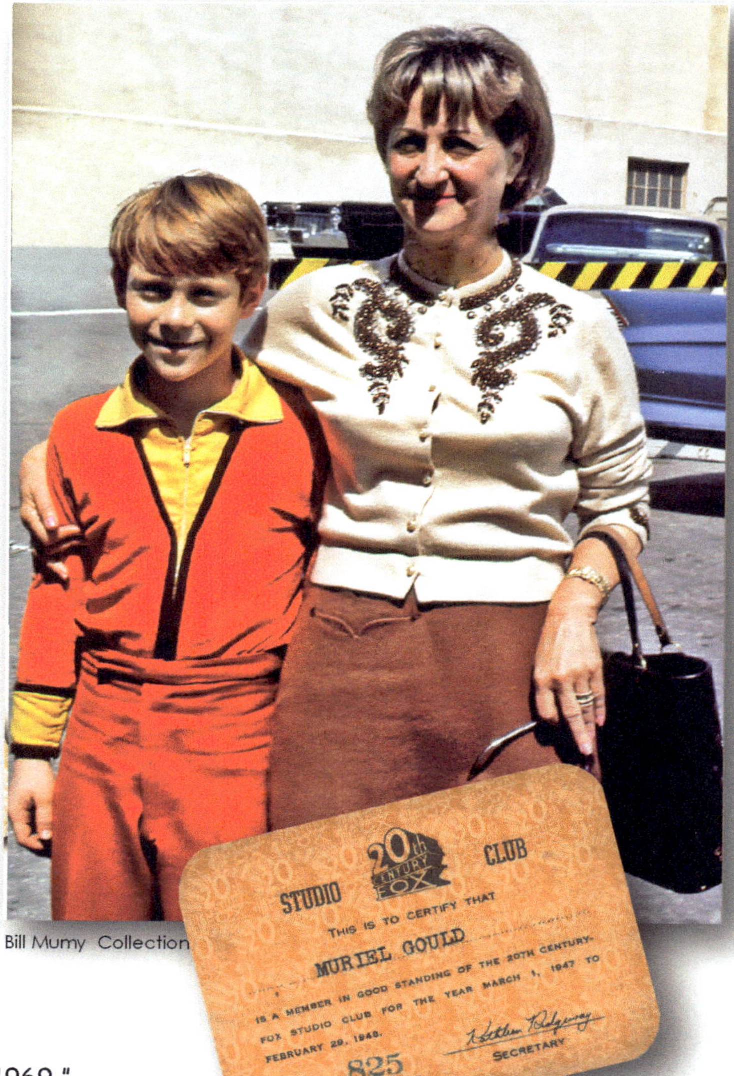

Bill Mumy Collection

"Here's a true story I've never told anyone before. It's a little tacky of me, but here goes... back when we were shooting the series, what is now known as Century City basically didn't exist. It was mostly just fields of grass and the Century Towers (where Jack Benny lived), the Century Plaza Hotel, the Broadway department store, and a Gelson's. Fox had sold off most of the backlot property after *Cleopatra*, but it would be years before it was really developed. The Fox lot was quite different then compared to what it became over the next half century. In the mid-1960s, the publicity department was simply a double banger trailer out on the grass standing alone on the Avenue of the Stars. The entire department was run by a very nice guy named Jet Fore. Cool name, right? Well, Jet would often ask me to come over to the trailer and sign a stack of promo photos for normal studio publicity stuff (here's where the 'entrepreneurial' part comes in)... my friend and neighbor Craig, was a year and a half younger than me attended public school like all my 'civilian' friends did. People knew he was good friends with me and they started asking him if he could get them my autograph. So, I started asking Jet if I could take a bunch of *Lost in Space* photos and pics of the various shows that he was promoting, like *Batman*, *Green Hornet*, *Voyage to the Bottom of the Sea*, *Time Tunnel*, etc. and also some scripts once in awhile too. Jet was totally cool about it and after I'd sign a bunch of promo stuff for him, he'd give me a stack of stuff. Then, I'd go around to the various sets when I had a chance to and I'd get my friends who acted on the shows to autograph them. Then, I'd give them to Craig who would bring a few at a time to school and he'd sell them to students at lunch. Then every weekend, Craig and I would split the money and we'd each have an extra 20 or 30 dollars to buy comic books with! In a way, we were pioneers of today's common autograph business. Of course in another way, we were kinda sneaky and maybe ran a bit of a hustle. Anyway, I never told that story before."
BILL

FYI The studios used to send out postcards to fans when they wrote in for an autograph. These are rare collector's items today.

Photos from Cartwright/Mumy Collections

DRESSING ROOMs

"My dressing room had a stereo record player in it. Everyone brought vinyl albums and would use my trailer as a music room when they had some spare time to relax. Mark liked Richie Havens and the soundtrack to *Stop The World - I Want to Get Off*. Marta brought in The Byrds and some Dylan. Ange was all about the Beatles and British pop. I was worshipping at the altar of The Kingston Trio, Pete Seeger, and Peter, Paul and Mary. Guy and June listened to soft classical music in one of their trailers. Jonathan was a real opera buff, but he didn't listen to music at work. He was too busy stealing the show!

The dressings rooms for me, Ange, Mark, Marta, Bobby, and guest stars were small trailers parked right outside the soundstage we were shooting on. The school trailer was there too. Guy, June, and Jonathan had nicer dressing rooms that were inside Stage 11."
BILL

Bill Mumy Collection

"My dad took this shot outside my trailer when he came to visit me during the filming of *Princess of Space.*"
ANGELA

Angela Cartwright Collection

"Those small trailers were pretty cool. They were like your own tiny apartment. Every morning your costume would be cleaned and pressed and laid out on the sofa which was just big enough to curl up in a fetal position to have a nap. Of course... I never took a nap. I was too busy in school, on the stage, listening to music, or eating lunch in our down time. There was a mirror and a small stool and just enough room to change your outfit. Our dressing rooms were practical, but not at all glamourous and the air conditioning in those days was bad."
ANGELA

Make Up For Lost Time...

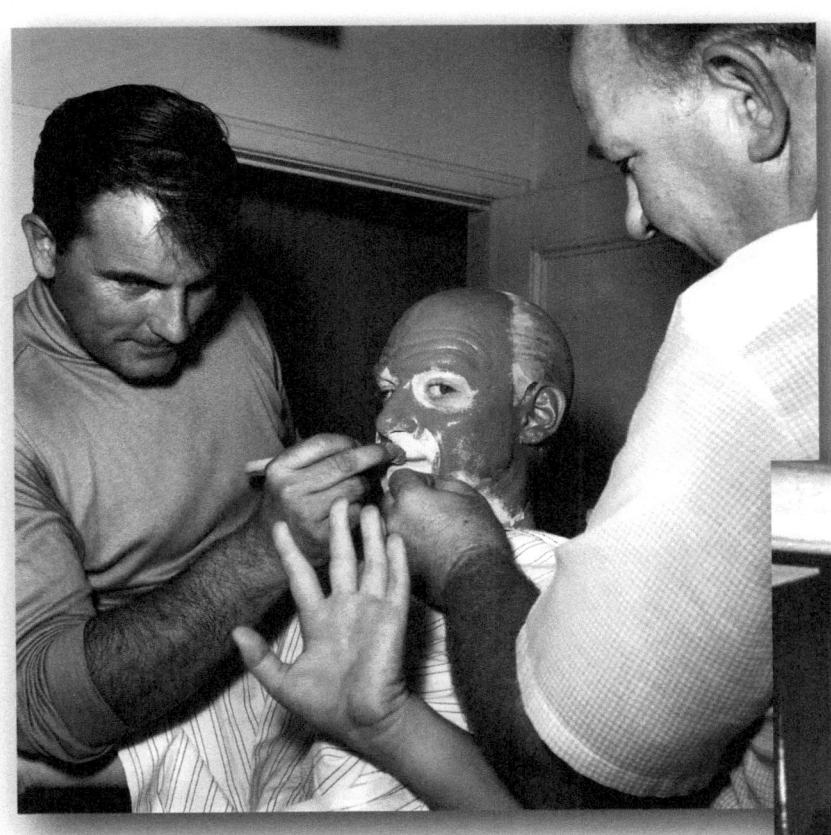

"Johnny Chambers, the iconic makeup artist who designed the *Planet of the Apes* makeup, created the 'Will becomes Smith' makeup for our Season 3 episode *Space Destructors*. They did a fantastic job. But the process wasn't pleasant. It took many hours. Having a life mask made where they cover your face in a clay-type compound that hardens while you breathe through two straws in your nostrils felt like being buried alive. It's a creepy, restrictive, smothering experience. Ahhh, how we suffer for art!"
BILL

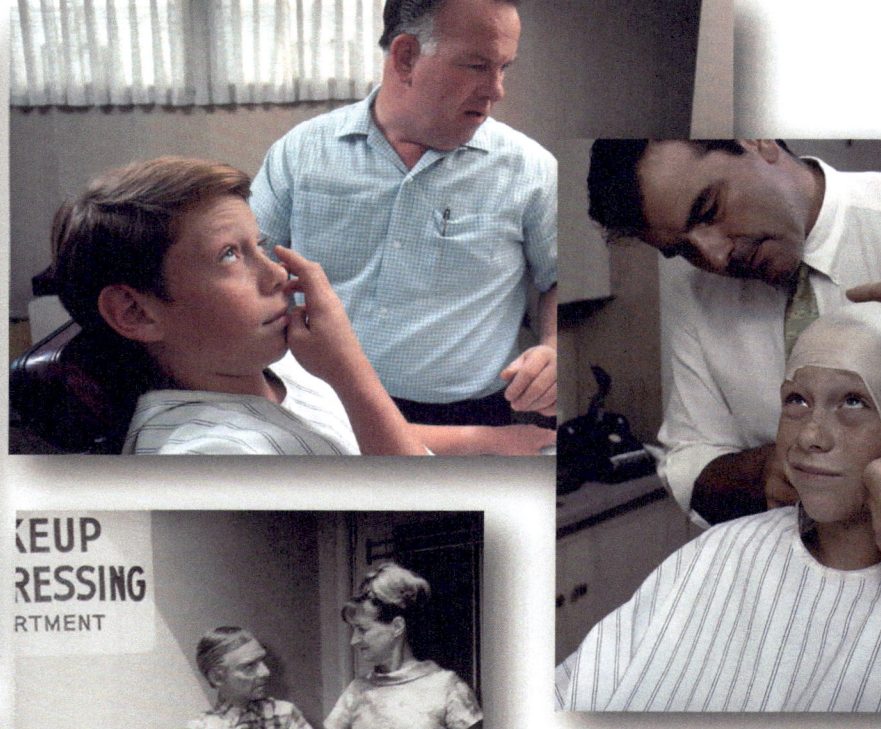
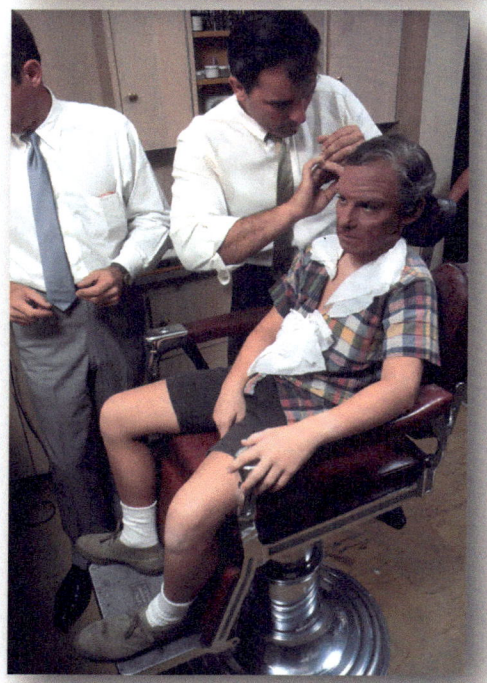

"In my mom's 1962 Jaguar Mark II, a very boss car, heading home for lunch where I scared the crap out of my grandmother."
BILL

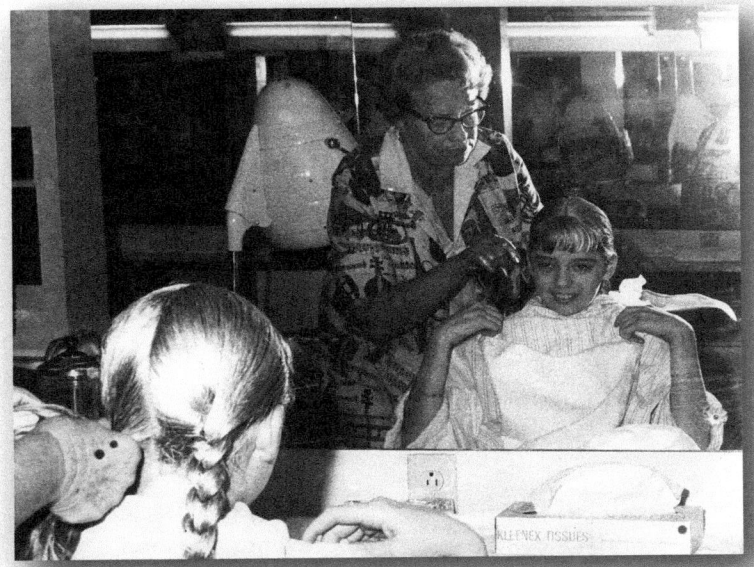

Angela Cartwright Collection

"You think acting is glamorous? Try sitting in a makeup chair for a couple hours while silver makeup is applied to your face and hair. For the record, I epitomized bling before it was popular in the episode *All That Glitters*."
ANGELA

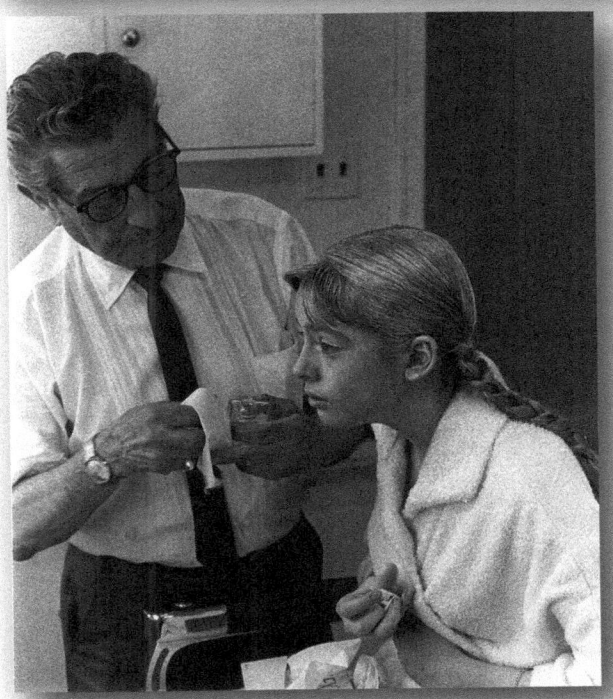

"The assistant director had called 'first team!' which means the camera crew has finished lighting the scene with the stand-ins and they're ready for the actors on the set. Inside Jonathan's dressing room, he and I check our looks before heading out to shoot."
BILL

"Marta freshens her lipstick while the hairdresser combs through my hair. When you're in showbiz you get used to people constantly fiddling with your hair, makeup, and wardrobe."
ANGELA

"This was June's way of walking from the stage to her trailer and stopping the elements from ruining her hair and makeup. It was a chiffon scarf, purple I believe. I remember that sign beneath her name on her dressing room door. I wonder who put it there and the story behind it."
ANGELA

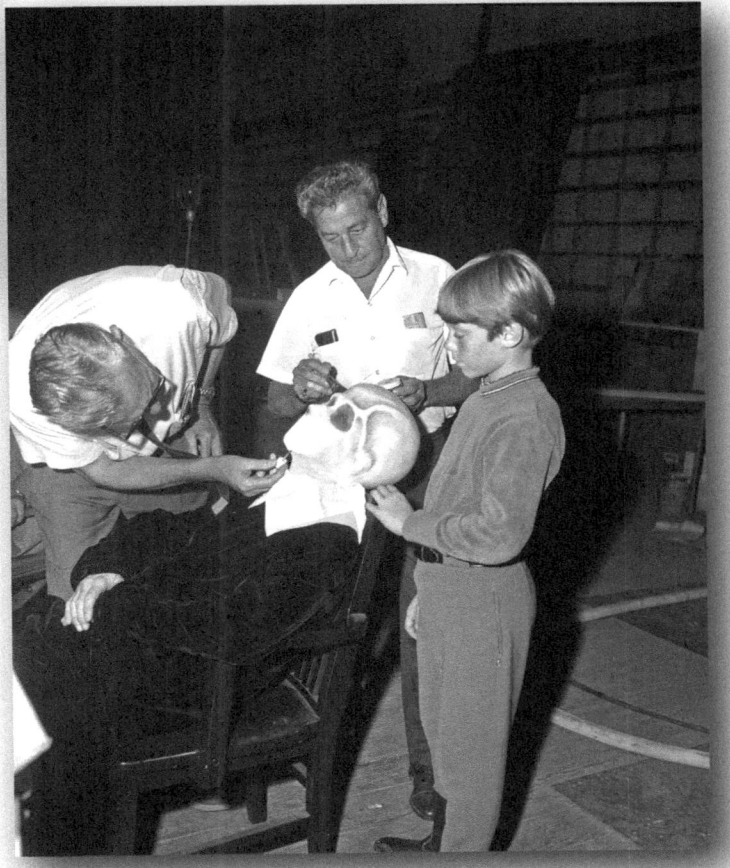

"This makeup completely covered this alien's mouth. I don't think I could have endured that."
BILL

"While doing some hair tests for the episode *Princess of Space* I was sitting in the show's hairdresser chair when I heard this intense buzzing in my head. Much to the hairdresser's dismay I couldn't help shaking my head to get the buzzing to go away. It turned out a gnat had flown into my ear and was driving me quite crazy. I was whisked off from the set to the mini-hospital on the lot that was a few steps away from the Old Writers' Building. The nurse in charge, who was nicknamed Band-Aid, came to my aid and put something in my ear that froze the intruder so she was able to pull it out with a Q-Tip.

I remember thinking how could something so tiny make such a loud noise (this, mind you, was before I had children).
The little mini-hospital on the lot used to practice medicine in a very country-style way. Anything that needed major medical care was sent to Cedars-Sinai Hospital. But for a twisted ankle, a bandage for a cut, or a gnat in your ear, Band-Aid came to the rescue and this was the place to go. To this day, I pull my hair over my ears before I go to sleep."
ANGELA

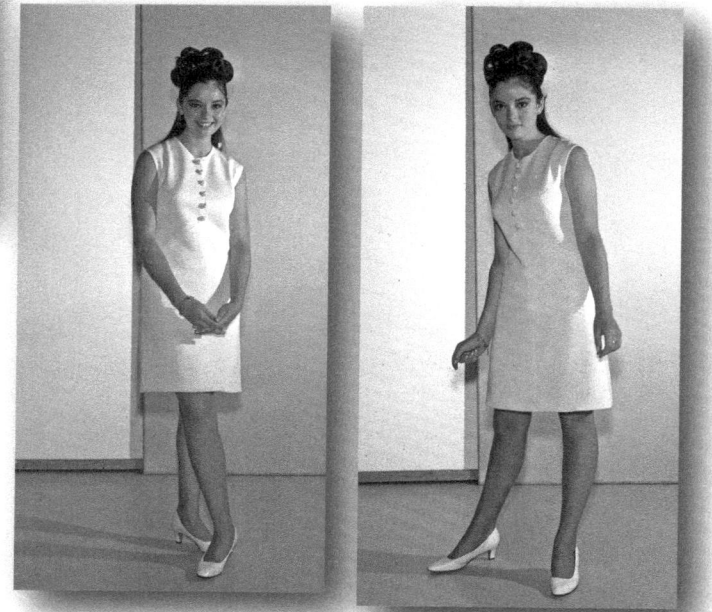

"For an uplifting experience I always wear heels when shooting continuity hair tests. These shots were for my up-do in *Princess of Space*." ANGELA

"The thing about crying on camera for me, it wasn't always difficult, but... once you'd done it, really cried, in a master shot, it was tough to get the tears to flow over and over again for closeups. Off times, a makeup artist would step into the frame just as the camera started to roll and they'd blow a little menthol in your eyes and/or place a few glycerin tears on your cheeks. Hey, we can't all be Meryl Streep all the time!"
BILL

A Sticky Situation

"I remember what it was like to sit in the hairdresser's chair every morning and have DEP slathered on my head to keep all the little wild hairs from popping out. On would go the DEP and a comb would be dragged through it leaving little comb lines. Then my hair would be tied tightly back with a rubber band. I was used to it, having been Linda Williams every week on the *Danny Thomas Show* for seven years. A ponytail was synonymous with my character then and it had spilled over into Penny Robinson. Irwin had told me he was a huge fan of Danny's show and I think what he really wanted was Linda in space. Needless to say, I shampooed every night and I hate anything sticky in my hair to this day."
ANGELA

"I was pretty happy with my look in the third season of the show. I sported eyeliner and my groovy new mini skirt. I started off the third year with my hair (which reached down my back to my butt) long and flowing, but word came down from Irwin that my hair looked 'like a shawl' and the powers that be asked me if I would cut it. I said I wouldn't be very happy if I had to do that, and the next thing I knew I was wearing a little half wig, a pageboy kind of thing, that was a much more conservative style of the time. Even though it had me sitting in the makeup chair for an hour every morning while they braided my real hair and pinned it under that hairpiece, I was glad they had found a solution. I don't think I was ready for my long hair to be chopped off at that time."
ANGELA

"My Silky Terrier, Sgt. Pepper, and my new hairdo for Season 3."
ANGELA

WARDROBE

"Paul Zastupnevich was the costume designer on Irwin Allen's productions. Paul Z, as we fondly called him, was a visionary. I'm pretty sure it was Paul's brilliant idea to pop those colors onto the television screens the year we switched from black and white to color. He wanted each character to have their own color so you could recognize them from a distance. Paul Z even had spacey names for the colors he used, like meteor red, solar yellow, asteroid green, orbital purple, and jet pink. I think he called my Season 3 costume comet green. There was not a show on television at that time which had that primary rainbow look. It was like we stepped into a Peter Max painting. He was a creative and all-around sweet guy."
ANGELA

FYI Paul Z also dressed Angela in the *1979* Irwin Allen movie production of *Beyond The Poseidon Adventure*.

"This picture was taken between the pilot and the first season. Irwin Allen was upset that I had cut my hair after the pilot. No one has been upset about me cutting my hair since."
BILL

"Oh those first season suits were so uncomfortable. They were heavy canvas suits and if you bent your elbow, it cut off the circulation to your arm. They were a pain to walk around in and unbearably hot. I was so relieved when a new fabric called Metlon-with-Mylar, an aluminum fiber coated with Mylar, replaced the heavy cardboard-like suits. Even though they were still hot, they moved with your body and were much more becoming on our girlish figures. This picture is obviously taken during a rehearsal as my Velcro flap is unfastened and you can see the meteor red lining."
ANGELA

"The new suits were much more comfortable and easier to move around in, but in my opinion the original ones looked a lot better on film."
BILL

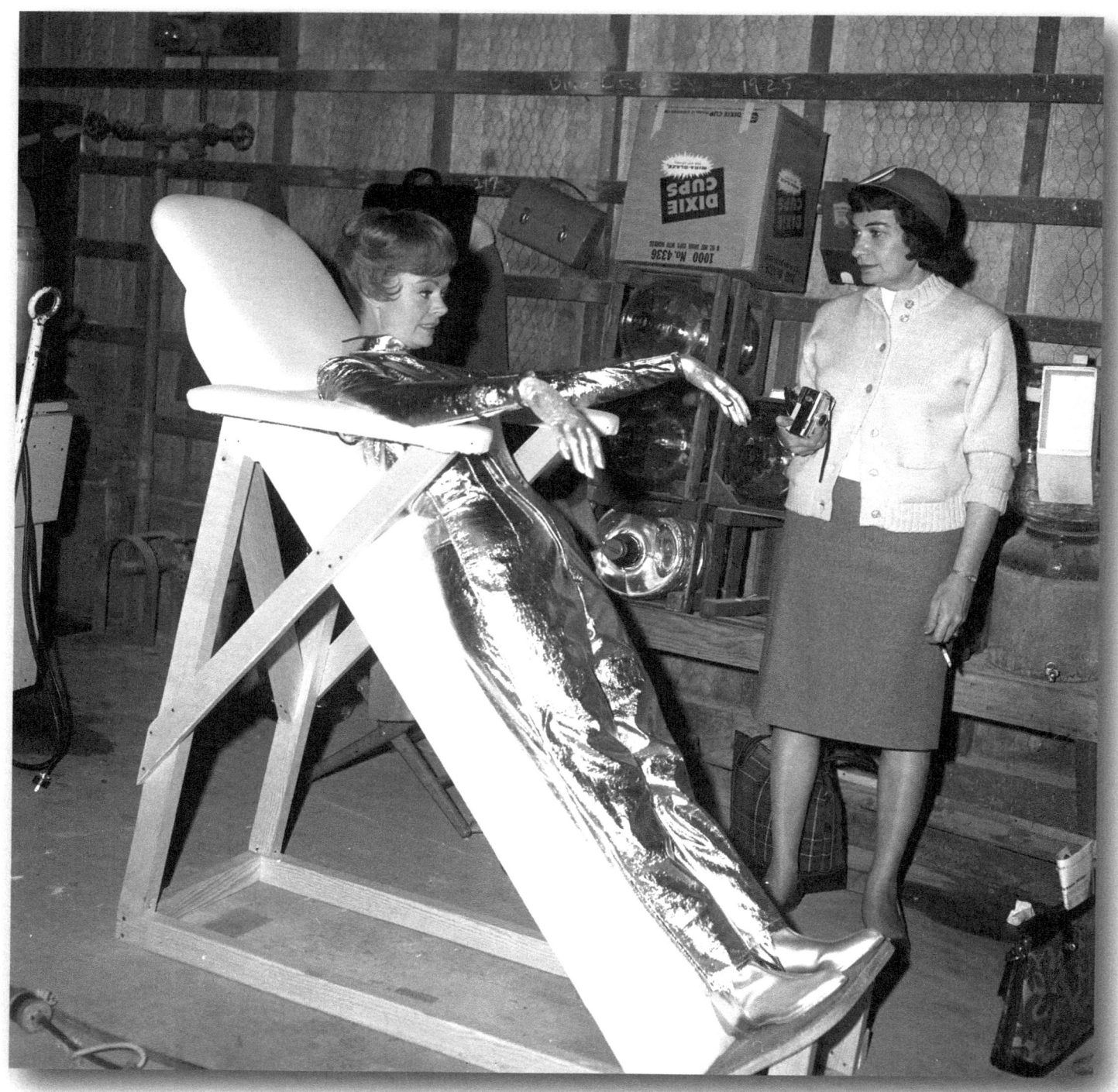

"The slant board was invented for actors in period costumes and formfitting tight dresses to rest between takes when their wardrobe was restrictive. For Season 1 our wardrobe was so uncomfortable and the slant board was shared with everyone."
ANGELA

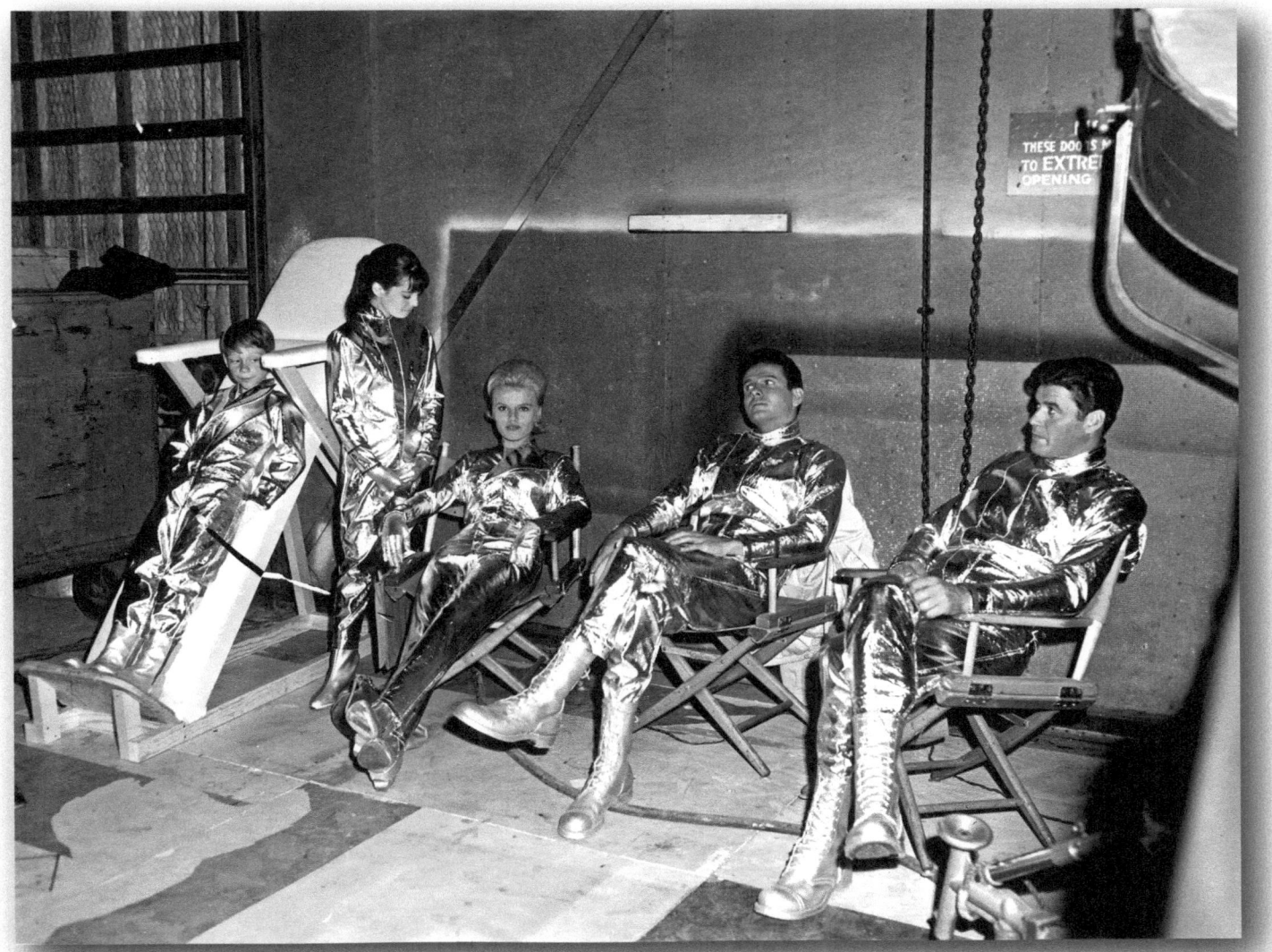

"Ange and I had more costumes than everyone else, because we grew so fast. Everyone had three copies of each change. One was for stunt people and two for us. Paul Z was always making us new ones as we'd outgrow 'em."
BILL

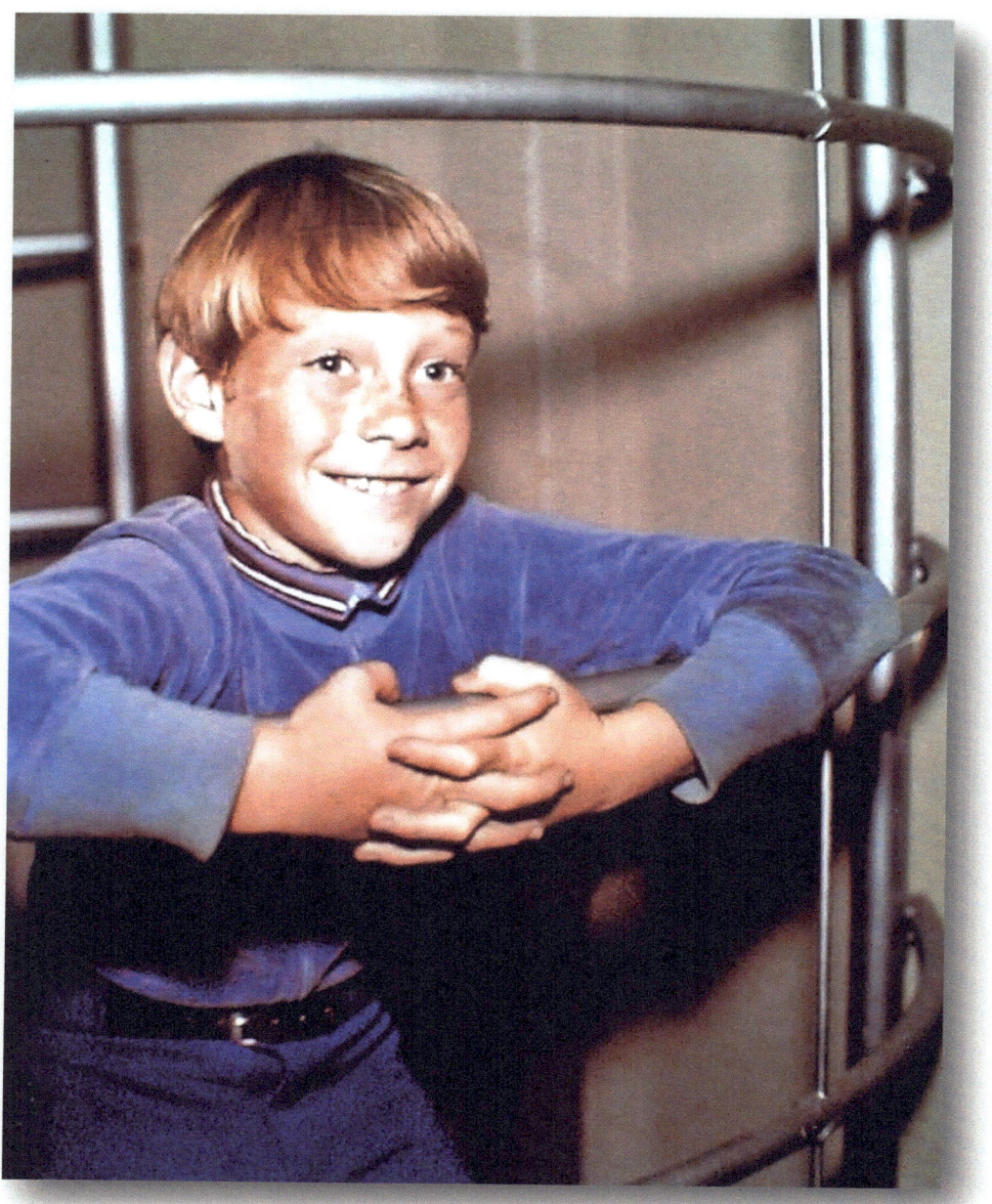

"We all had quite a few costume changes over the years, but I always felt they got it right the first time. My original navy blue outfit with red trim was, and remains to this day, by far my favorite. It's a bummer you can't get good velour anymore!"
BILL

"I loved my mint green short swing tunic. It was a sign of the times, the swinging 1960s. Mini skirts, knee high boots, and colors like you were popping off a comic book page."
ANGELA

"A Paul Z sketch for a Bill Mumy third season costume that never came to be. And Paul's drawing for my third season outfit where the design was kept but the colors were changed."
ANGELA

"Was it just a coincidence that my Brigitta von Trapp play clothes that I wore in *The Sound of Music* would be almost the identical fabric that my *Lost In Space* parka was made out of? Was Paul Zastupnevich a *Sound of Music* fan? Inquiring minds want to know, but I doubt we ever will."
ANGELA

Julie Andrews and Angela filming *The Sound of Music* in Salzburg, Austria.
Angela Cartwright Collection

WARDROBE TEST SHOTS

"I love wardrobe test and continuity photographs, because they were never meant to be seen by the public. These photos often give the viewer a true glimpse behind the scenes. No actor really likes taking these photos but they are an essential help to the wardrobe, hair, makeup, and camera departments to be able to view the characters and review how wardrobe, makeup, and hair for this character is going to look on film. As you can imagine, I was thrilled to uncover these wardrobe images from the show."
ANGELA

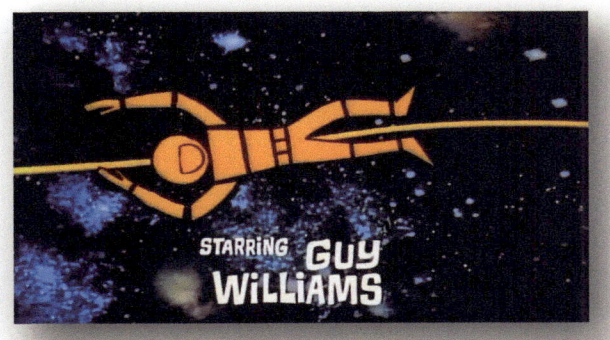

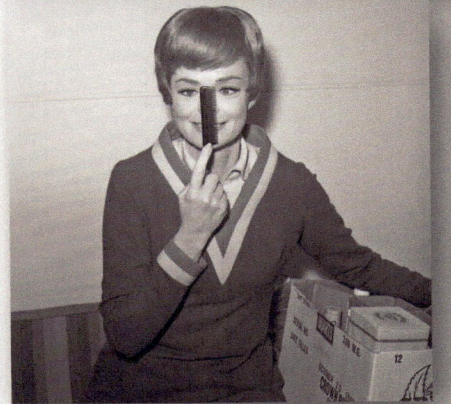
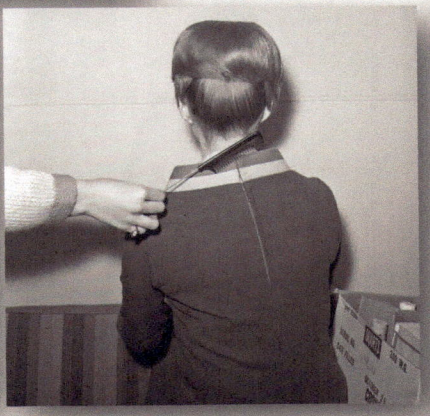

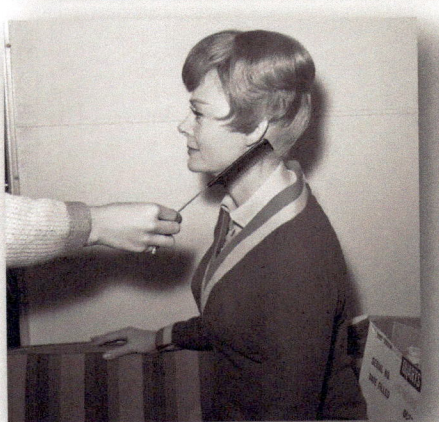
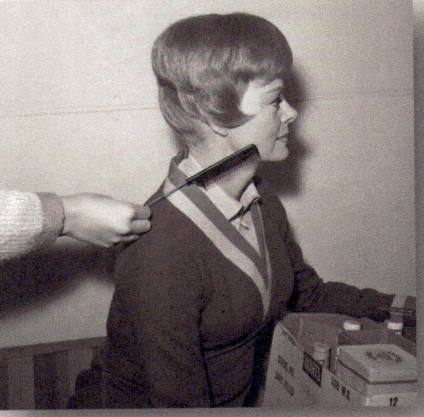

"The comb in these images means these photos are meant for the hair department, so they can see a hairdo from all sides and recreate it every day."
ANGELA

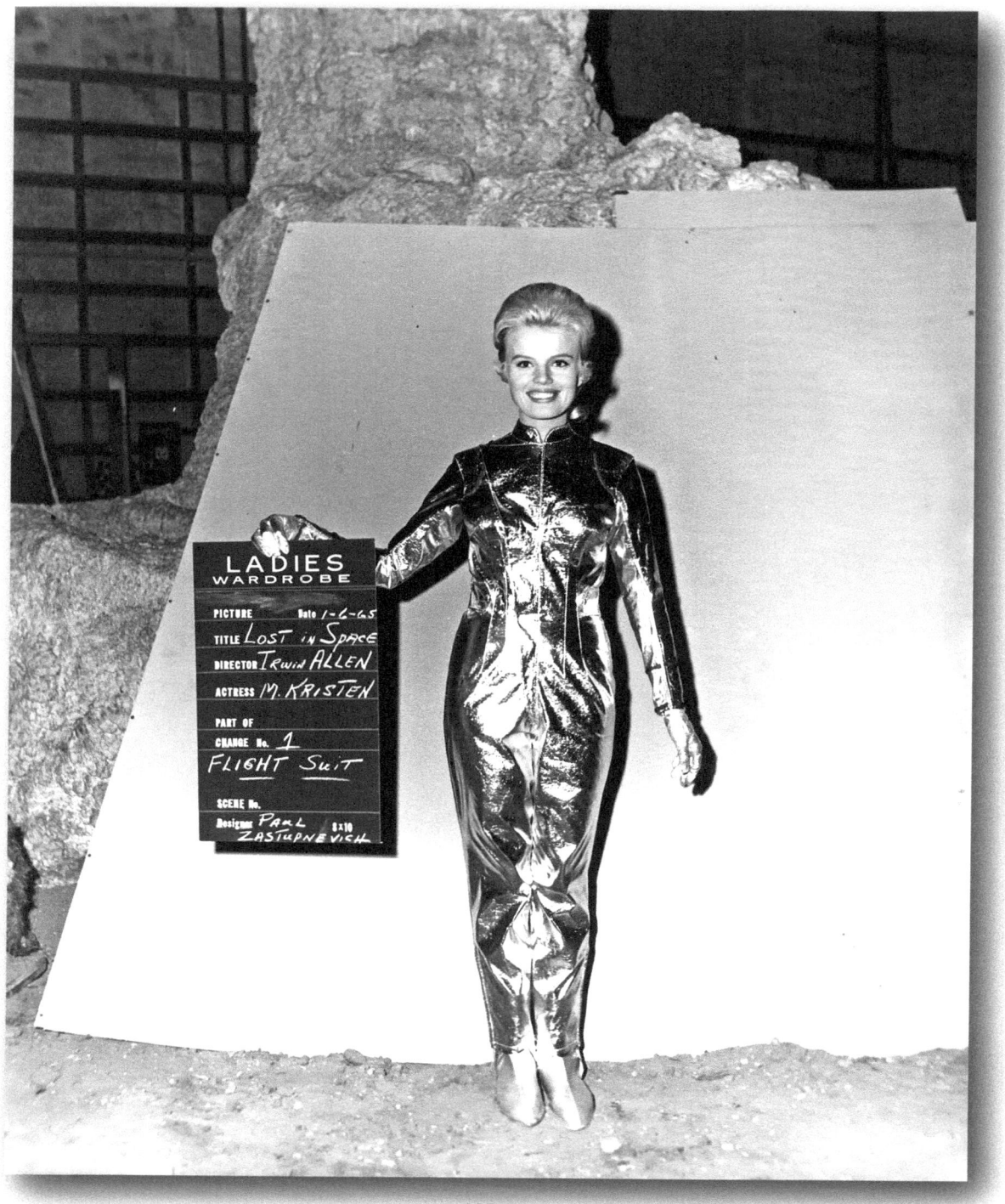

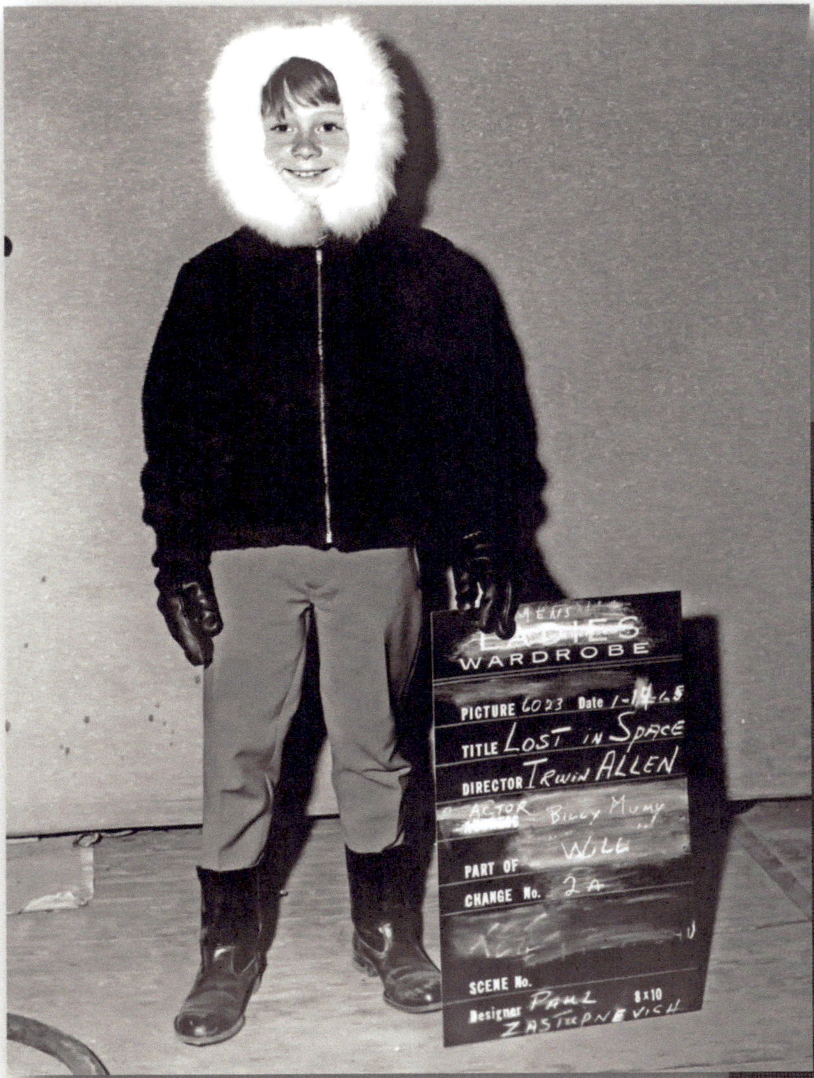
LADIES
WARDROBE
PICTURE 6023 Date
TITLE Lost in Space
DIRECTOR Irwin ALLEN
ACTOR Billy Mumy
PART OF WILL
CHANGE No. 2A
SCENE No.
Designer PAUL ZASTUPNEVICH 8x10

BILLY
MUMY

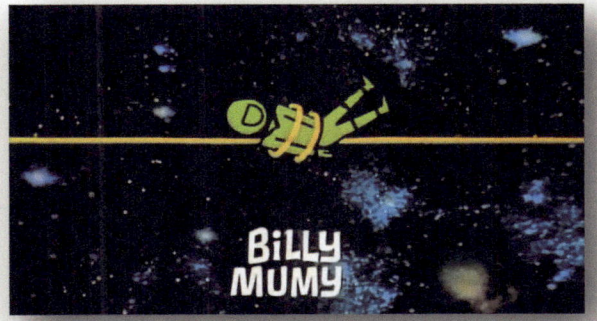

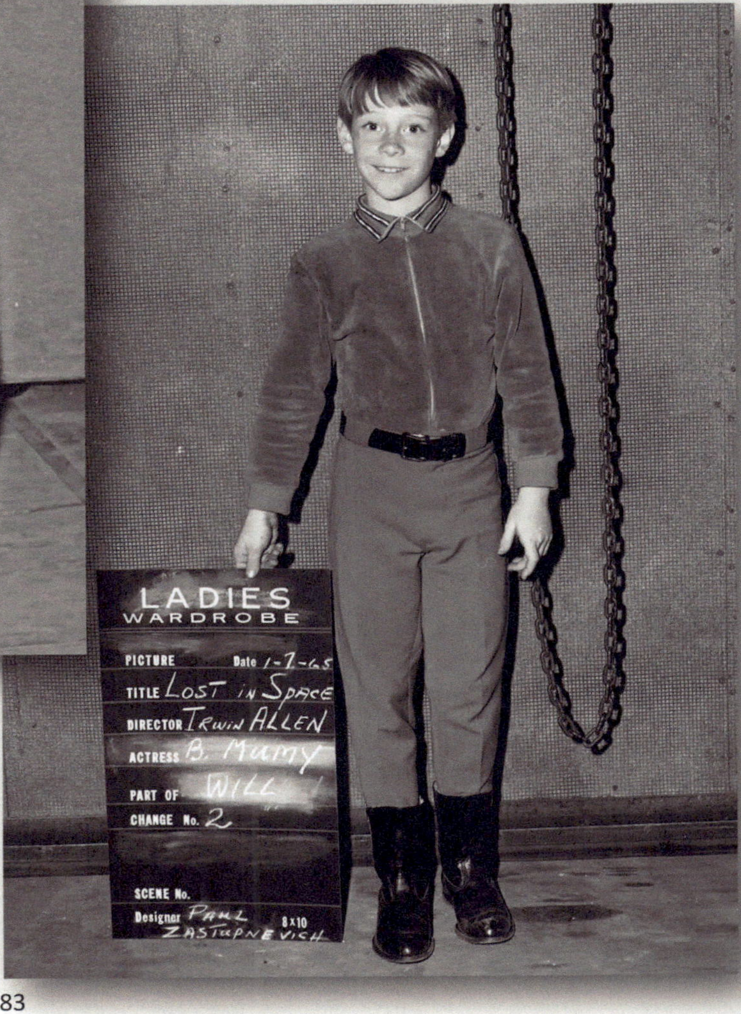
LADIES
WARDROBE
PICTURE Date 1-7-65
TITLE Lost in Space
DIRECTOR Irwin ALLEN
ACTRESS B. Mumy
PART OF WILL
CHANGE No. 2
SCENE No.
Designer PAUL ZASTUPNEVICH 8x10

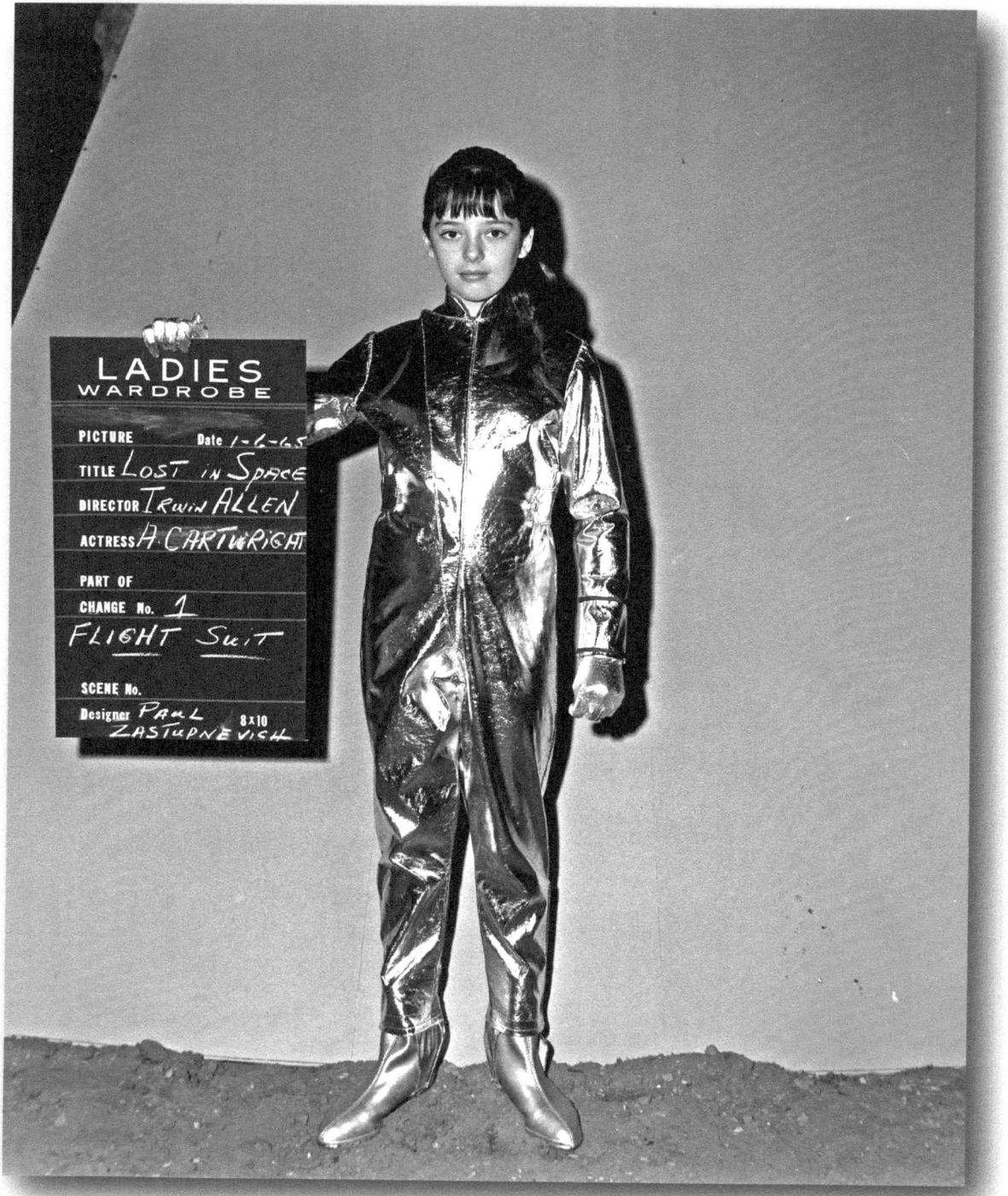

"Jonathan was a powerful teacher in many ways. I'd worked with many iconic legends before he and I became the team we became, but 'Himself' and I spent literally years in front of the cameras together and as time passed he shared some important lessons with me that I'll certainly never forget. Jonathan was all about getting it right straight off. He told me he always showed up 15 minutes earlier than his call time and I've tried to follow that example ever since. Like an upstanding scout, Jonathan was always prepared. Before he and I would be called to the set as 'first team' to shoot a scene together, he would request of the school teacher that I be brought to his dressing room a few minutes early so he could discuss the tone of the scene with me as well as teach me my NEW cues, because he always rewrote Smith's dialogue!

Brains are so amazing and they work differently for everyone I guess. One thing that Jonathan could do, that I never could do, was remember everyone's name. He knew the name of the stage hands from regional plays he did back in the 1940s. His memory for names was incredible. My memory is really good for dialogue and song lyrics and certain trivia, but I'm terrible at remembering names.

Another valued piece of wisdom from Jonathan was: 'Never deny a stunt person a check, Billy Person!' As a kid on *Lost in Space*, I was always happy to jump off a rock or be close to the explosions or tumble down something with debris falling all around me, etc., as long as the welfare worker approved. I was up for it, but Jonathan made a good point: 'If I let Sandy, my double, do it... she'd get a nice check.' Still as a young wannabe superhero, I did the bulk of Will's stunts. However a little over a year after wrapping up the series, Jonathan's advice echoed in my head when I was guest starring on an episode of the western drama *Lancer*. We were shooting an exterior scene where I steal Jim Stacy's horse and start to ride away, then he whistles, and the horse rears and bucks me off. They knew I was a seasoned rider and wanted me to do the fall. But I remembered what Jonathan had said and I told them I'd rather have the stunt man do it. Well, he did... and he broke his neck. It wasn't a permanent disability, but it was pretty scary. Thank you, 'Himself!'

Jonathan was so great. A true one of a kind. If he liked you, he pretty much loved you and he was generous and funny and wise and wonderful. And if he didn't care for you much, you became aware of it quickly. Jonathan, especially during his last 10 years or so, did not suffer fools."

BILL

BLOOP...BLOOP

"Debbie was very smart and patient. I know actors that would have complained about having to wear that headgear all the time, but she was a pro and only got cranky after she had worn it for hours at a time."
ANGELA

"I must admit, Debbie's kisses were strange, and I was the recipient of several of them during the course of the show. I remember that feeling to this day."
ANGELA

FYI The Ritter fan used to create cosmic storms can be seen in the background of this picture.

"The Bloop endeared herself to our audience. Legendary makeup artist Johnny Chambers used Debbie's face as a template for the *Planet of The Apes* makeup. Debbie also had a recurring role in the CBS TV series *Daktari,* a show about an animal behavior study center in Africa. She went on to star in the spy show *Lancelot Link: Secret Chimp* in 1970 as Mata Hairy. Debbie was a very busy working chimp."
ANGELA

"It wasn't often you would find Jonathan acting with and holding a scene-stealing Bloop. In fact, I believe this is the only time I remember."
ANGELA

"Debbie, the chimp who played the Bloop, was a sweetie. I really liked her and she loved Ange. I can feel her fingers in my mind right now. She was strong and had a very powerful grip. Her fingers were quite dry and her fur was somewhat coarse. She smelled a bit funky. She didn't enjoy having the Bloop headpiece strapped on her. I never felt nervous or uncomfortable with Debbie, but when I think back on it, with all the explosions, sparks, smoke, and chaos we dealt with in our episodes, it could have spooked her at any minute. Lou Schumacher, her trainer, was an okay guy. Times were different then. He could be a bit tough on Debbie. One day Ange's kid brother Christopher was visiting the set, he was about five or six, and for some reason, Debbie bit him on his finger. It wasn't a serious wound. The next time Debbie was on set, she had been de-toothed. That always bothered me and Ange. Debbie lived into her 30s. She spent her last years in the San Diego Zoo. I hope she was happy."
BILL

JUST MONKEYING AROUND

"Ears and no ears. I must say Debbie was most patient with that hot headpiece she had to wear."
ANGELA

FYI Most people know that Walt Disney himself supplied the voice for Mickey Mouse. Rumor has it that Debbie the Bloop was voiced by none other than Irwin Allen.

"When Debbie wasn't practicing her acting skills, she worked as a valuable member of the camera crew. But she really wanted to direct. >Bloop, Bloop<." ANGELA

Never Fear, Smith Is Here!

"Jonathan distributes canine kisses to my new pup Razz (short for Erasmus). Ange's Silky Terrier, Sgt. Pepper, awaits his turn."
BILL

"Jonathan would say, 'Angelinio, your parents have not come up with a suitable dowry for us to marry. Two goats is not enough.' I always got a kick out of that."
ANGELA

> **FYI** One of Jonathan's many talents was that he was a magnificent needlepoint artist.

"It would be years after the series ended that I found out Jonathan had a lovely wife, Gertrude. When I finally met her, she told us they liked to keep their careers separate. Gertrude was a major executive with Clairol and Vidal Sassoon. She also developed and marketed DEP hair styling gel. She once told us, 'We had red DEP for redheads... yellow for blondes... and blue for old ladies... but it was all the same crap. It was only food coloring, darling!' Gertrude was so lovely, I only wish I had known her longer."
ANGELA

"Jonathan and Gertrude were childhood sweethearts. They met in the Bronx when Jonathan was 12 and Gertrude was 13. 'She robbed the cradle!' Jonathan would remark. They were married for almost seven decades and had one child, Richard. Jonathan's passions were gourmet cooking, gardening, opera, cruises, and needlepoint. I am the proud owner of one of his fine needlepointed masterpieces."
ANGELA

Gertrude and Jonathan with their son Richard.

OH THE PAIN...

"Every day around 4:00 pm when sugar levels were low and there was a ton of work still left to do, Jonathan would hand out Tootsie Roll Pops to the cast and crew.
It was a ritual everyone appreciated at the 4:00 pm needing-a-pickup time. He must have bought those tootsie rolls by the case. However, Jonathan never did anything without purpose. He told me, 'Treat the crew well and keep them happy and they will always make you look your best on camera.'
I never forgot those wise words."
ANGELA

"Not to be outdone by Jonathan's daily sweet treats, one day after lunch at Duke's near the studio, Mark showed up with a 20 lb bag of peanuts and climbed up the catwalk high above the set and started throwing peanuts at the cast and crew. Oh that Mark, what a character... always made us laugh every day."
ANGELA

Favorite 'Smithisms'

Bubble-headed booby
Blithering bumpkin
Neanderthal ninny
Cantankerous clump
Computerized clod
Pot-headed prankster
Lily-livered lump
Nervous ninny
Ramshackle Romeo
Gargantuan goose
Parsimonious puppet
Hard-headed harbinger of evil
Ill-informed ignoramus

ANCIENT ALIENS

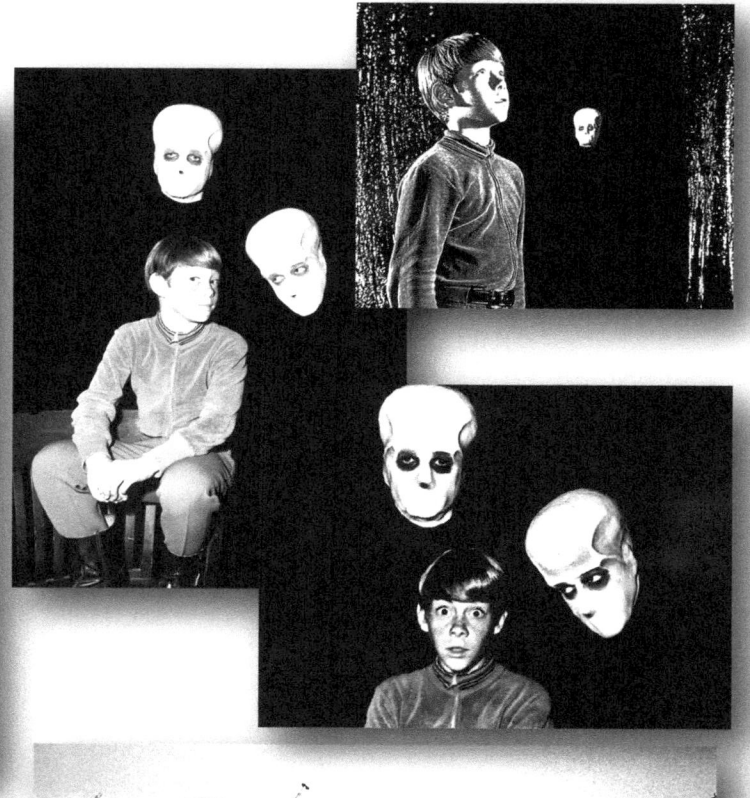
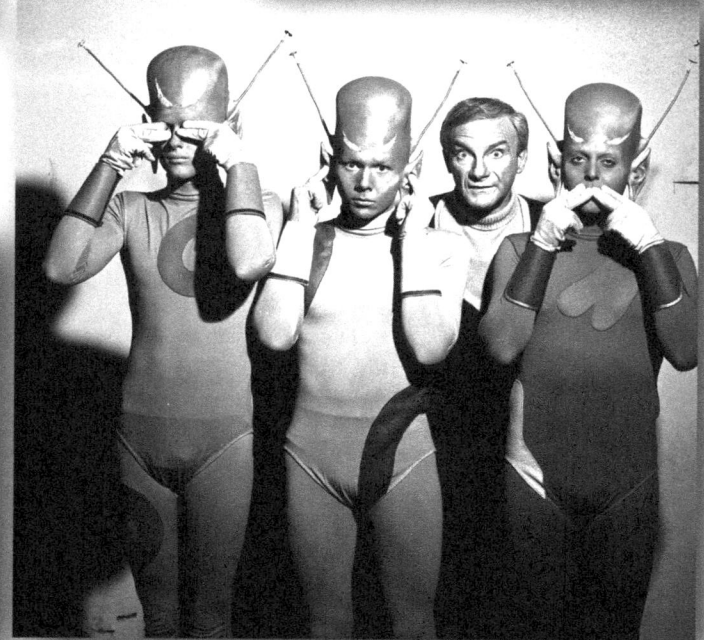

"There was no question aliens existed on our show weekly. Wait a minute, that's a Robinsons' laser gun never used by the Golden Man. See how you can't trust everything you see and read."
ANGELA

"Nothing like a little attitude in space."
ANGELA

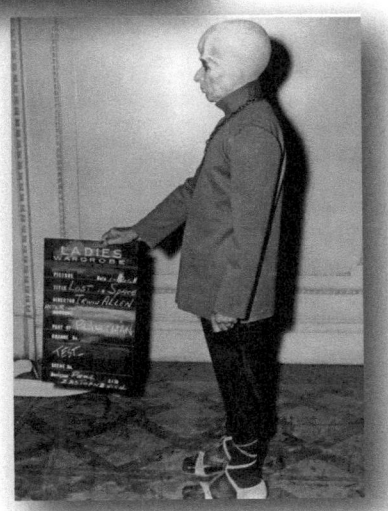
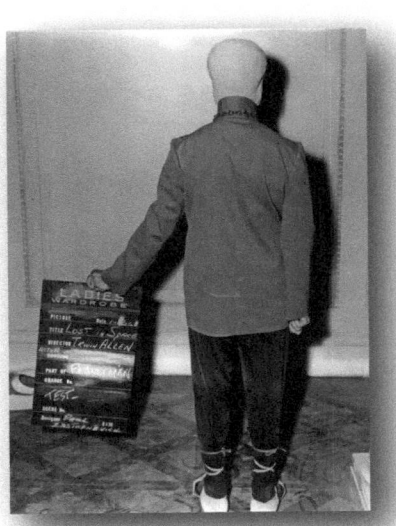

COLLECTIBLES...

LOST IN SPACE
WE PLANET THAT WAY

"Over the years there have been hundreds of officially licensed *Lost in Space* merchandise products. There are books and websites devoted to all of that minutia. This is not one of them. What you see on this page is the rarest of the rare: in-house promotional buttons and stickers that were never distributed to the public. These were made by Irwin Allen and 20th Century Fox just for fun. They have survived for 50+ years inside my officially licensed *Lost in Space* lunchbox. How rare are they? This *Lost in Space: We Planet That Way* bumper sticker is the only known one left in the world."
BILL

From the Cartwright/Mumy Collections

FYI A rare vintage postcard complete with printed cast signatures that the studio would mail out to fans who wrote in.

"Only two people had the *It Computes* bumper sticker. Kevin Burns and Bill."
ANGELA

From the Cartwright/Mumy Collections

Guys and Dolls

"I was very excited to be a Penny Robinson action figure. She came with a laser gun and a Bloop. Not many people can say that. People may be action figures, but not everyone has a Bloop!

Two Brigitta von Trapp *Sound of Music* dolls by Madame Alexander. One with a book and one in a dirndl.

A rare *Lost In Space* Penny doll complete with freezing tube from Japan.

My 12" Linda doll was $2.00 and 2 cereal box tops. She was available in toy stores in three sizes and the tallest one walked while you held her hand. She was very clever."
ANGELA

Angela Cartwright Collection

"It's good to be multiple action figures. It's real good."
BILL

"Multiple Wills, including a very rare vintage freezing tube one from Japan, and Anthony Fremont from *The Twilight Zone* in black and white and another in color."
BILL

"Lennier from *Babylon 5* in three different outfits. He was quite the fashionista."
ANGELA

Bill Mumy Collection

"Most of us had nicknames on the set... Jonathan called Bill, 'Billy Person'. Bill called Jonathan, 'Himself'. Jonathan always called me, 'Angelinio.'"
ANGELA

FAKE NEWS

"This has bugged me for years, so I'm setting the record straight here. This is not a picture of me riding on the large tortoise with the Bloop - that's a stuffed animal, not the Bloop - and more importantly, that's not even me! This was shot in the Mojave desert when they filmed the long shots of the jet pack flying when Guy was rescuing me and takes off again. It was filmed with stand-ins. But what I never understood was why would they use this picture in a trading card deck?"
ANGELA

PENNY'S PETS

Angela Cartwright Collection

POSTER KIDS

"A sign of a powerful artist is when you see his or her work and immediately recognize who made it. Juan Ortiz is among those whose signature style is quickly recognized by those who view it. I'm a fan."
BILL

"I love the art of Juan Ortiz. In his 1960s style Juan created a poster of every *Lost In Space* episode. They are all extremely cool. These are two of the portraits from his collection which can be found online and in his book *Lost In Space: The Art of Juan Ortiz*."
ANGELA

CAN ANYONE HEAR US SCREAM?

"I was a pretty good screamer. It felt good to scream once in awhile. Sometimes for the publicity shots they would ask us to look like we were screaming, or look scared. You just did it, never for a moment thinking that 50 odd years later you would be looking at those images saying... 'Man, are those ever dumb.'"
ANGELA

No residuals?!?! Arrrgghhhh!!

Fire In The Hole...

"You could say I've always carried a torch for the series."
BILL

"Our on-set teacher was on high alert when we shot these episodes with fire and explosions. Just off-camera I remember the firemen with extinguishers at the ready."
ANGELA

I'VE GOT MY EYE ON YOU

"Here is Paul Z holding a John Robinson action figure that was to be used in a scene where the cyclops grabs John mid-air. How cool would that have been? The scene was shot but then deleted, and sadly the footage has not been found. This is one of the rare shots taken inside Stage 5."
ANGELA

> **FYI** Lamar Lundy who played our alien giant cyclops was considered one of the best defensive ends in NFL history. He played for the Los Angeles Rams for 13 seasons. He was a member of the Fearsome Foursome alongside Merlin Olsen, Deacon Jones, and Rosey Grier. But he was no match for Will Robinson's laser gun.

"Irwin had another show filming on Stage 10 right next door to us, *Voyage To The Bottom Of The Sea*. *Voyage* and *Lost In Space* used to trade monsters. Our aliens could be seen painted and slightly altered to become sea monsters. Here, David Hedison, of the Seaview, does battle with our giant cyclops from the pilot. Irwin was well-known for being a great recycler before recycling became popular."
ANGELA

"For Season 3 we suddenly discovered we had a spacepod! It gave us the opportunity to travel in small groups without having to take off in the Jupiter 2."
ANGELA

FYI The numbers on the side of the spacepod, 277-2211, are the actual phone number of the 20th Century Fox studio's main line and the IA stands for Irwin Allen.

"With any free time I had, my dad and I were always shooting photographs in our garage studio and developing them in the dark room. One time my dad found this old helmet that worked perfectly with my spacesuit.

Photos by John V. Cartwright

Another time my dad created this whole Jupiter 2 set with some old electronic equipment he'd found. I have to giggle when I see this shot of me in front of our vaporizer standing in as a spaceship. With some white shoe polish on a piece of glass he created a galaxy. He was a real MacGyver with an endless imagination and I loved our creative photo shoots."

ANGELA

THE CROWN...

"I loved dressing up in my princess regalia. It was great to shed those space costumes we wore week after week and walk around in a fancy dress and heels. While I personally prefer a tiara, my dentist told me I needed a crown. I was like, I know, right?"
ANGELA

Rocking and Rolling...

"I can still hear Irwin pounding on his metal wash pail with a hammer so we could lurch from side to side in unison. It did keep us rocking and rolling when dodging comets or falling rocks during earthquakes, though Irwin's method was a bit primitive."
ANGELA

"When we started the show Marta was several inches taller than me. By Season 2 I had caught up with her. By Season 3 I overtook her... that's what happens when you are a growing kid on a series."
ANGELA

As I Was Saying...

"It's true that Guy was unhappy about the way the tone of the series changed and how his starring role became a supporting one. Who could blame him? Agents called producers, etc. and compromises were negotiated. However, and I can't stress this enough, there was no hostility or bad vibes between any of the cast members on our set. Guy and Jonathan, although never super close, always got along fine. They were true professionals."
BILL

Visitors on the Set

"It wasn't unusual for guests to visit the set and we'd often pose for snapshots with them in between setups. I have no idea who Jonathan and I are smiling with here. What's cool about this photo, to me, is you see both Sandy Gimpel and Handsome Harry (stand-ins and stunt doubles for me and Jonathan) in wardrobe behind us. I'm pretty sure something was about to blow up in the next shot."
BILL

"For the kids who watched our show every week, visiting our set was like a trip to an amusement park. The spaceship loomed large on Stage 11 and walking on the sand where aliens had set foot, was a treat indeed."
ANGELA

"On this day, Guy's family (Steve, Toni, and his wife Jan) had a special meeting with Debbie the Bloop."
ANGELA

A Galaxy of Guest Stars

"Kurt Russell was working all the time as a kid actor, and we crossed paths quite often. Then he guest starred on our show. It was fun to say 'Why you conceited dirty-faced little boy, you're nothing but a bully, a half-pint bully.' In real-life, Kurt is nothing like that at all."
ANGELA

"We had a ton of outstanding guest stars on our show, including famed character actor John Carradine. It's hard to walk onto a set as a guest star and work with a group of people who have been together for several years, but that's all part of it."
ANGELA

"Looks like Strother Martin brought his *Blast Off Into Space* wardrobe hat from *Lost in Space* to his iconic performance as Percy Garris in *Butch Cassidy and the Sundance Kid*."
BILL

> **FYI** Sheila was with Irwin until his death November 2, 1991 and continued to take excellent care of all of Irwin's projects until her death November 15, 2013.

"Sheila Mathews was cast by Irwin for three episodes, *Return From Outer Space*, *The Space Vikings*, and *Princess of Space*. Sheila was sweet. Jonathan loved telling the story of her whispering to him at her wedding to Irwin Allen 'Got him!'. Then Jonathan would say, 'She earned it, every morning she had to wake up and there <u>it</u> was.' We think he was kidding!?"
ANGELA

"Ahh, the glamour of showbiz. While filming this scene with Jonathan, in *The Space Vikings*, Sheila was munching and then tossing huge turkey legs off camera. What she didn't know was that after the first take, the prop men picked the discarded food up out of the sand, brushed it off, and used the same pieces for subsequent takes, resulting in gross mouthfuls of sand and turkey. But, being a trouper, she didn't complain."
BILL

"I had worked with Al Lewis on an episode of The Munsters the year before we started Lost In Space. Working with him and Jonathan on our show was a trip. I felt like the cheese between two pieces of ham!"
BILL

"Not many people know that Guy was a serious tournament chess player. Fritz Feld was also an avid chess man, and he collected photographs of himself on various productions playing chess with his acting colleagues. June is probably distracting Guy as well as cheering him on in this pic."
BILL

FYI Fritz Feld had worked with Angela in *The Danny Thomas Show* as the mouth-popping Chef Marcel in three episodes in 1960-1962.

"Michael Rennie starred in *The Keeper*, the only two-parter we ever did. Many fans consider this episode a high point of the series." ANGELA

FYI Michael Rennie was reunited with Jonathan whom he had co-starred in the 1959-1965 BBC television series *The Third Man* (which ran for 72 episodes).

"Passing the time by playing Boggle with Wally Cox during the filming of Season 2." BILL

"On my list of favorite episodes is *The Magic Mirror*. I loved the whole creepy concept, but it makes you wonder what our writers were smoking."
ANGELA

FYI Lou Wagner, who played J5, an impish potential love interest for Penny in Season 3, lived three doors down from Bill in Laurel Canyon for many years. His custom-built house looked like a castle.

FYI Before Michael J. Pollard went on to fame and received a *1967 Academy Award nomination for best supporting actor for the role of CW Moss in Bonnie and Clyde, he guest starred in *The Magic Mirror* episode as a lonely boy attempting to lure Penny into his isolated dimension. It *originally aired February 16, 1966.*

"Albert Salmi, who played the dynamic space pirate, Alonzo P. Tucker, was one of my favorite guest stars to work with. I thought we had nice chemistry together and the episodes he appeared in remain favorites of mine. In real life, he had a very tragic ending, but I remember him fondly."
BILL

"Francine York as the noble Niolani in *The Colonists* was perhaps the first dominatrix in space. Dee Hartford was cast as Nancy Pi Squared in *Space Beauty* and twice as the android Verda."
BILL

SIX DEGREES OF SEPARATION, OR LESS.

"During the run of *Lost In Space* I was reunited with several of my former cast-mates. Like Sherry Jackson in the episode *The Space Croppers*, who for years played my big sister Terry on *The Danny Thomas Show*.

Hans Conreid appeared as Sir Sagramonte in the *Lost In Space* episode *The Questing Beast*. Hans appeared in 23 memorable episodes as Danny's boisterous Uncle Tonoose in *The Danny Thomas Show*."
ANGELA

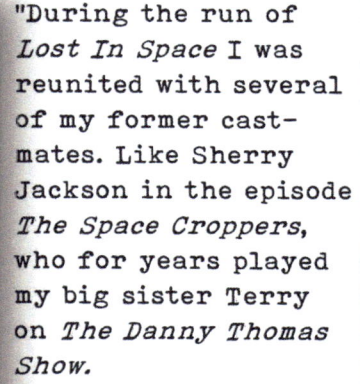

Angela Cartwright Collection

Angela Cartwright Collection

"My little sister Gretl in *The Sound of Music* was played by Kym Karath, who was cast as a Princess in *The Last Civilization* episode. Bill was to give her a kiss that awakened the Princess, but I have no idea why he's kissing her in the school classroom. I guess they were rehearsing?"
ANGELA

Heather Menzies, Angela, and Kym Karath during filming of *The Sound of Music*.

"I worked with Kym, first in *The Sound of Music*, then in *Lost In Space*, and then I went on to work with Heather Menzies (my sister Louisa in *The Sound of Music*) in her TV series *Logan's Run*. In those days it was a small world after all."
ANGELA

Color photo from Angela Cartwright Collection

Sounds of Music...

Paul Hornsby, Angela, Bill, and Gregg Allman on the 20th Century Fox lot and with Duane Allman at the Whisky a Go Go.

"What an incredible decade the 1960s was! Everything was constantly changing in big ways. Fashion, music, politics, etc. June Lockhart appreciated opera and classical music very much, but she was also tuned into the very newest and most happening rock bands of the day. June hired Duane and Gregg Allman's band, Hour Glass, to play a private party she hosted. They were signed to Liberty Records at the time and were just starting to get a buzz going (in more ways than one!). The Hour Glass wasn't quite as blues-oriented as the Allman Brothers Band. They were more of a psychedelic hard rock group, kinda like Iron Butterfly, but more R&B as I recall. Anyway, we went to see them play at the party, then June invited the band to visit us at the studio. June also took Ange and me to see them play at the Whiskey a Go Go on the Sunset Strip. They opened for the Nitty Gritty Dirt Band. It was a fun gig. I wore a Nehru jacket and talked guitar stuff with Duane in the dressing room. Ange looked amazing as usual. All the band members were drooling over her."
BILL

Photos from Bill Mumy Collection

"In 1965 the Beatles were
at the Hollywood Bowl.
Bill and I were invited. I
went and had a fab time.
'Yeah! Yeah! Yeah!'
But Bill didn't go...
Carpe Diem my friend...
Carpe Diem."
ANGELA

Angela Cartwright Collection

Photo by Angela Cartwright

"There was a CBS party where I got to
meet the Beatles before the concert. I
found this pic I took while waiting to
meet the Fab Four. Standing in front
is their publicist Derek Taylor and
their roadie Mel Evans behind."
ANGELA

FYI In a recent book about the Beatles tour of the USA, it mentions how they used to watch *Lost in Space* in their hotel room to pass the time.

"I remember thinking, 'Who wants to hear 15,000 screaming girls listening to 'Yeah, Yeah, Yeah'... I was a folk music snob at the time. I dug the Beatles but passed on going. I stayed home and listened to the Kingston Trio. It's one of my top five regrets of all time. Every time I see this photo I could kick myself all the way to Alpha Centauri, cuz I know I should be right next to Ange. Oh well, let it be... hang down your head Bill Mumy, hang down your head and cry."
BILL

"While we were still filming the series Bill and I made an appearance at Super Circus at the Pan-Pacific Auditorium on November 23, 1967. After our singing performance, Bill and I were chased in the parking lot by a bunch of fans. I remember thinking 'This is right out of the movie *A Hard Day's Night*,' and WHAM, I ran right into a thick cable guide wire that was holding up the tent. It knocked me off my feet and I was out cold. I don't remember anything after that.

I had a concussion a couple of weeks later while we were filming a *Lost In Space* scene. The whole cast was standing listening to the director and I felt my head starting to spin. I recall pulling on Bill's sleeve and saying 'I'm going to faint, I'm going to faint' and Bill saying, 'Yeah, yeah', and then... I fainted. I've only fainted once in my life, and that was it. I don't remember if 'the show must go on' was applied or if they sent me home. But I do remember taking this picture right before I went on stage to sing *Rain* and Bill sang *Mr. Spaceman*."
ANGELA

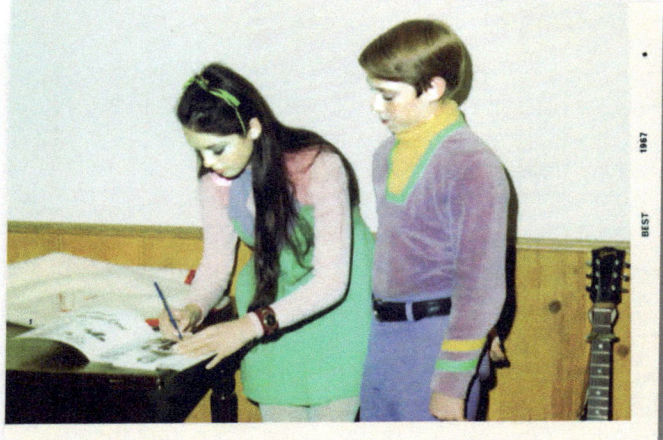

Angela and Bill signing programs at Super Circus, 1967.

Photos from Cartwright/Mumy Collections

"Following the Three Stooges was tough! But, I did my best. I sang *Mr. Spaceman* by The Byrds and my own song, *I Hear the Train*. We did a lot of personal appearances while we filmed the series. Parades, charities, telethons, TV and radio shows. Super Circus was a lot of fun until Ange got knocked out by a guide wire. Then it got very serious and intense and scary. Everything can change in the blink of an eye."
BILL

Photos from Bill Mumy Collection

"The very first musical gig I ever played in my life was to a sold-out crowd at the Hollywood Bowl. Ange and I were there to promote the series. It was the summer of 1965, Scout Day at the Bowl. The place was packed with Boy Scouts, Girl Scouts, Cub Scouts, and Brownies. The event was hosted by Art Linkletter. I was pretty nervous. The song I performed was *Tijuana Jail*, an old Kingston Trio tune about going down to Mexico, getting drunk, gambling, and being thrown in jail with no way out. You would have thought that either my parents, or some publicist, or Art Linkletter, or anyone in a power position would have recommended I play something a little 'tamer' for the kids... such as *This Land Is Your Land* or something... but no one did. So my song of choice was *Tijuana Jail*, what can I say."
BILL

"I can't believe we all wore our costumes. Bill and I sure took one for the team since those are the first season spacesuits."
ANGELA

Bill, Angela, and Veronica Cartwright with Sally Field, there to promote her TV series *Gidget*.

Photos from Bill Mumy Collection

"I remember this performance at the Hollywood Bowl. It was a packed house. My sister Veronica and I sang *Ain't No Mountain High Enough* and I guess I knew how to play it on my guitar. Then Veronica sang a solo *Cotton Candy* while wearing her Jemima Boone prairie dress costume from *Daniel Boone*. I closed our performance with *Let There Be Peace On Earth* by Sy Miller and Jill Jackson-Miller. I was one of the first to ever sing that song, but it has since been recorded by many iconic artists. I remember thinking Bill's choice of a song was a weird one for that performance. But I guess singing in our spacesuits that day was pretty weird too.
ANGELA

Photos from Angela Cartwright Collection

"We were kept very busy. Here are a few shots from a personal appearance I made in Raleigh, North Carolina during the third season. Occasionally I'd fly to another state for a weekend to promote the series and I'd play a short set of songs and then sign autographs and usually do some radio, press, and local TV interviews as well.
I wore those gold corduroy pants a lot back in those days. I was a young troubadour."
BILL

"We were often asked to give awards and attend various events. This was an appearance June and I made during the last season of *Lost In Space*. (Left) A singing performance at the Hollywood Bowl before the first season of *Lost in Space*."
ANGELA

Photos from Cartwright/Mumy Collections

WE ARE CUT OUT FOR THIS JOB

"When we were on hiatus, visitors and tours would come and visit our soundstage. These pictures were taken as we posed for our life-size cutouts that were placed around the set for tourists to see. When the show ended we probably ended up in a dumpster on the lot. What a shame...
Not everyone is cut out for showbiz."
ANGELA

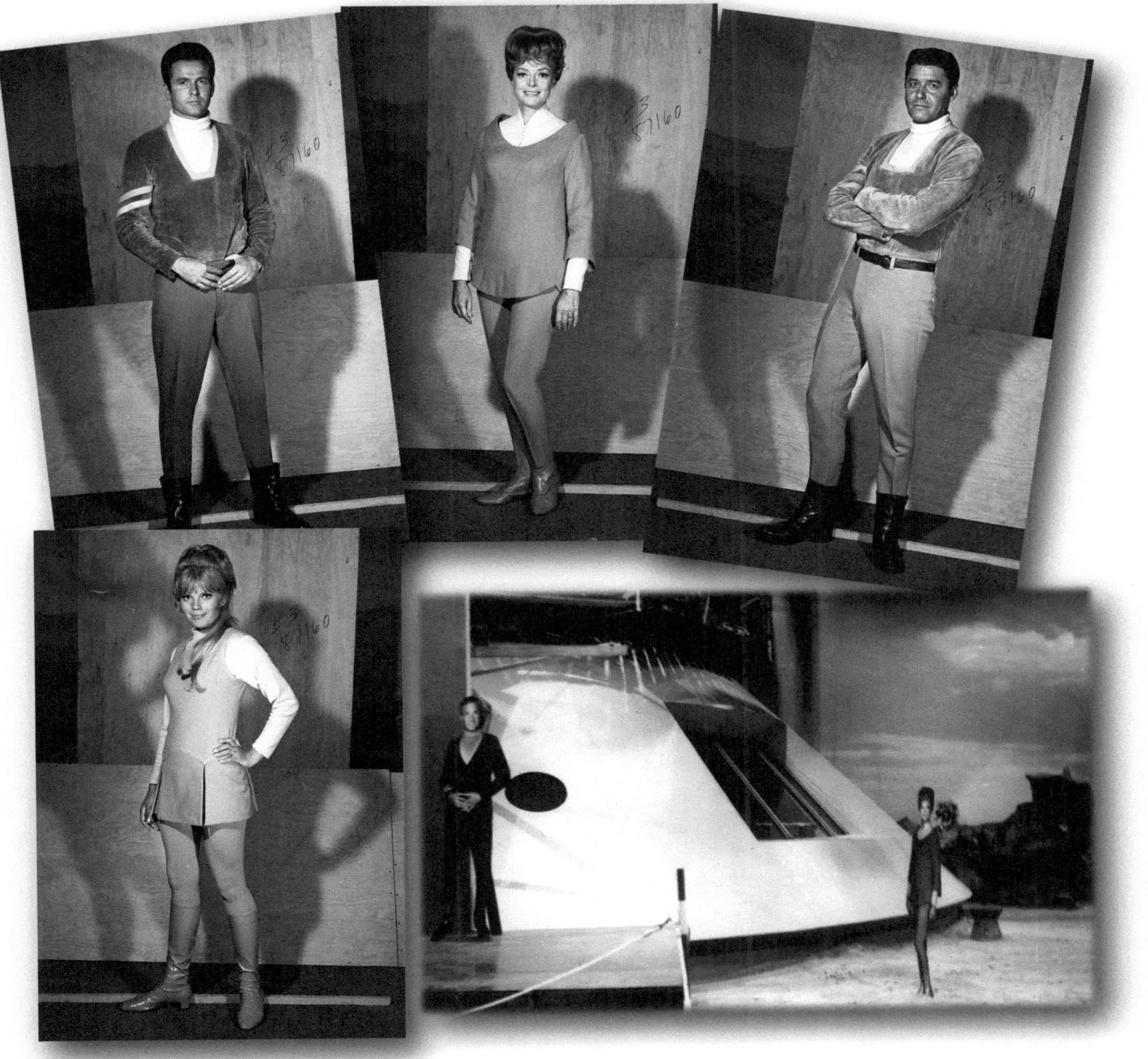

"Mark and I are saying A-OK for no reason at all."
ANGELA

"These newly found photographs have uncovered many images we have never seen before. Like this one on the right from Season 3, and this rarely seen strange outtake photo below with Guy holding my face and everyone laughing. I'd seen it before but tried to forget it. It's so odd."
ANGELA

SCHOOL DAZE

"Because we were minors, we could only be at the studio nine hours a day (nine and a half if they gave us a 90 minute lunch). A typical day was nine to six. That included three hours of schooling, lunch, and filming. Our schooling had to be completed by 4:00 pm and we had to have it in increments of no less than 20 minutes at a time. We still found time to goof around and explore the vast Fox lot."
BILL

"Frances Klampt was the permanent 20th Century Fox school teacher. She started that gig when she taught Shirley Temple from her first film on. She educated all the child stars who worked at the studio from the 1930s through the 1970s. Frances was and remains a very big and positive influence on both of us. She encouraged our creativity and also made sure our normal school curriculum was met. She always looked out for us. Bill and I both loved her."
ANGELA

Bill, Frances Klampt, David Jolliffe from *Room 222,* and Angela.

Color photo from Bill Mumy Collection

"I can't remember why we were using the galley set as a schoolroom, but it's fun to see my old notebook! I used to visit Jet Fore, who worked in publicity on the Fox lot, and he'd give me stickers the studio made to promote their shows. Besides Linus Van Pelt front and center, there's a complete set of Fox promo stickers to be studied on my blue cotton notebook. The teacher in this photo was a substitute, and her name escapes me now."
BILL

"I could walk or ride my purple Schwinn Stingray bike to the studio from my house, it was so close (and I did when we were on hiatus and just there for school). That was cool."
BILL

FYI Bill still has that purple Stingray to this day!

Color photos from Bill Mumy Collection

"Shirley Deckert was our on-set Season 3 school teacher. She was easygoing and forgiving of my antics. She taught me how to self-hypnotize myself. I had a stye in my eye from the sand on the set. I went to the doctor to have it lanced. They offered me anesthesia and I said 'That won't be needed, I will hypnotize myself to feel no pain.' They cut my eye and I fainted from the pain.
Thanks, Mrs. Deckert."
BILL

Photos from Bill Mumy Collection

"When the series didn't return for a fourth season, as we'd all expected it to, Ange and I hadn't made arrangements to go to other schools, so we were allowed to stay in school on the lot with Frances Klampt as our teacher in the Old Writers' Building. Ange is a year and four months older than me. So, when she got her driver's license, I suddenly felt embarrassed riding my purple Schwinn Stingray bicycle to school. For awhile, I rode a Honda motor scooter, but it was borrowed, so I started walking. Pretty soon Ange started picking me up every morning in her shiny new white Chevy Camaro. That was nice. A few years later we both ordered new Camaros together. She stayed with white, and mine was a burnt orange Rally Sport model. Our license plates were 156 CPT and 159 CPT."
BILL

"Here we are inside our schoolhouse and outside by the Old Writers' Building with Stephen Arngrim from *Land of the Giants* and Darby Hinton from *Daniel Boone*. If you were going to school in the permanent schoolhouse you never knew who would be in school with you from one day to the next, as kid actors making guest appearances often joined us for school there."
ANGELA

Photos from Bill Mumy Collection

"On the lawn outside our schoolhouse on the Fox lot and on the steps on New York Street and in front of the Old Writers' Building. With Howard Rice from *Room 222*, Stefan Arngrim from *Land of the Giants*, and our lovely teacher Mrs. Frances Klampt."
BILL

Photos from Bill Mumy Collection

Happy Halloween

"June's Halloween parties were always fun. Gregory Peck lived next door and gave us an apple as our treat. I thought that was lame. But June always had a banquet of sweets."
ANGELA

"I was invited but stayed home to listen to the Kingston Trio. Some people never learn."
BILL

Candid photos from Angela Cartwright Collection

"Stepping out in Renaissance garb. Don't ask us why."
ANGELA

GALACTIC CHRISTMAS

"Here we are feeling very happy at a holiday party in one of the trailers outside Stage 11 with June, Guy, Mark, Marta, and one of our directors, Sobey Martin. Whatever anyone would suggest to Sobey, he'd reply in the positive with, 'better, better.' But he pronounced it, 'bettuh, bettuh.' He was a nice man, but he honestly fell asleep in his director's chair fairly often."
BILL

Original Vintage Christmas Card, circa 1965.

"Jonathan used to tell a story about Irwin Allen and the Christmas gift. Paul Zastupnevich did all of Irwin's holiday shopping for him. Their relationship was similar to Mr. Burns and Smithers on *The Simpsons*. One December night after a long day of shopping for the boss, Irwin called Paul back into his office and told him he needed to make one more trip to the store before calling it a day. Irwin decided Paul should buy a men's sweater. Cashmere, but not too expensive. The color didn't matter. Whatever caught Paul's eye would be fine. Wearily, Paul went back out shopping and eventually returned with a nice new cashmere sweater. Irwin inspected it and approved, adding, 'Now wrap it up nicely, Paul.'

After Paul had tightened the bow and finished wrapping the gift, he handed it to Irwin who handed it right back to him saying, 'Merry Christmas, Paul.' Nothing like that personal touch."
BILL

STUPID STUFF WE HAD TO DO

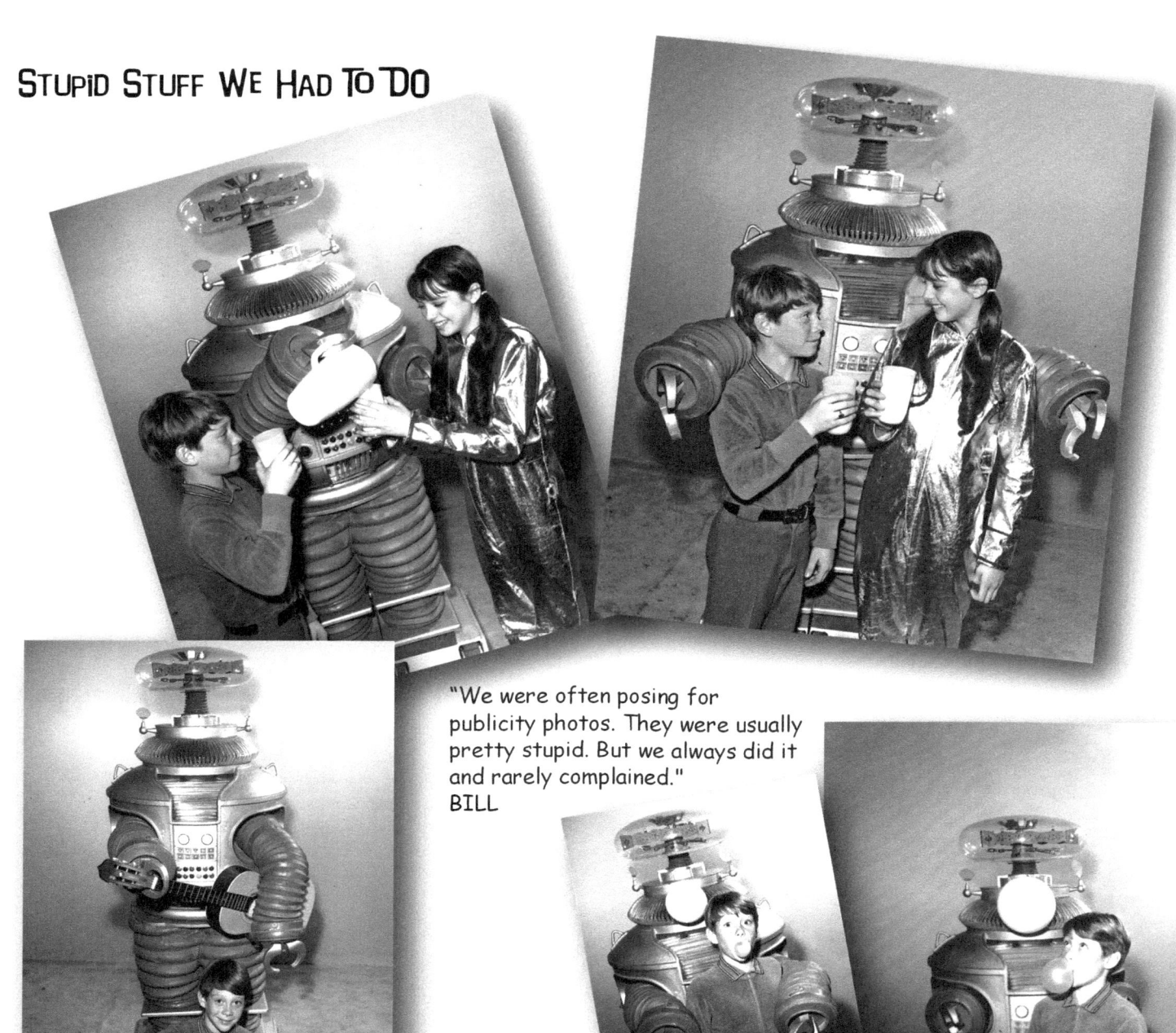

"We were often posing for publicity photos. They were usually pretty stupid. But we always did it and rarely complained."
BILL

"As if ONE Bill Mumy was not enough!"
ANGELA

"Here it looks like Bill's pants were lost in space, and he looks quite pleased about it."
ANGELA

"I hated posing for publicity photos out of character, but we did it all the time. In 1967, I became a certified scuba diver and most of my hiatus time was spent in the ocean either scuba diving, snorkeling, or body surfing. However, despite what these photos imply, I never owned a surfboard or surfed. I wore my own diver's watch on the series for most of the entire run."
BILL

FYI The Cartwrights and the Mumys went to Hawaii during the 1966 hiatus, but they went to separate islands.

Angela Cartwright Collection

"The studio put the fear of God into both of us with this photo shoot. I still have this Bible and Ange still has that prayer book."
BILL

"Here I am with my son Billy."
ANGELA

It Does Not Compute!

FYI Jonathan was frequently missing from the studio cast photos, but thanks to some digital wizardry, he finally made it into these group shots... better late than never!

Classic Mumy Captions

Don: "Don't make me throw Will at you Smith!"

"Kinky in Space."

"Things on the set got horny from time to time."

Don: "I'll take care of Sherry Jackson, Will. You don't need to worry about that. Just don't tell Judy."

"June gathered us together to take this goofy photograph in response to Mad magazine parodying *Lost In Space* with their brilliant *Loused Up In Space* and sent it to the magazine. Many years later, Kevin Burns 'added' Jonathan and the Robot to the image and had it colorized. A fun memory. Mad magazine #104 July 1966 was written by Nick De Bartolo and illustrated by Mort Drucker."
ANGELA

FYI Angela appeared in another Mad magazine parody called *The Sound of Money* #108 January 1967 written by Stan Hart and illustrated by Mort Drucker.

"People want to hear gossip and salacious stories. But the truth is, there simply isn't much of that to tell. Lost in Space was a very pleasant and professional environment. Sure, some actors had issues with the direction the series went in, which certainly wasn't what they had expected when we shot the pilot. But nobody ever stormed off the set in a huff. Everyone in the cast got along with each other very nicely. I'm sure agents made phone calls to business affairs on their behalf, but there were never any temper tantrums or actors refusing to come out of their dressing rooms on our show.
People think Jonathan Harris was single-handedly responsible for the shift in tone. The fact is, because of our time slot, 7:30 on Wednesday nights on the CBS network, it was the network that insisted the more realistic and darker tone of the show be changed to a sillier style because they aired us in the family hour and they didn't want anything broadcast that might scare little kids.
It's true that Jonathan himself started adding comedic bits to the character of Smith, and yes, Irwin Allen approved of that, and yes, Jonathan rewrote almost all of Smith's dialogue, but the main directive for change in tone came directly from the network.
In truth, I suppose the juiciest Lost in Space hookup tale in reality was me and Ange. Five years after we started the show, she and I became a couple for a few years. First loves. Then we broke up and didn't see each other for about 15 years and now we're very close pals again.
I'd like to tell you the details of the torrid affair between the Bloop and the Robot, but I signed a confidentiality contract about that."
BILL

Photo by John V. Cartwright

Lust in Space

"Edy Williams was quite a character. Everyone who was at the studio in those days will likely remember that she used to flash her boobs to the crew while they were building the Hello Dolly exterior sets. She appeared in an episode of Lost in Space, one of the goofier ones, Two Weeks in Space. One day on Stage 11, she took me aside and stuck her tongue in my ear and squeezed my crotch. I was 13. I can't say I liked it much. Whatever. Now you know."
BILL

"June and Guy were close. They were the same age and enjoyed similar things. Each had two children about the same ages. They enjoyed good wine, classical music, and reading. They spent a lot of the time together. The chemistry was undeniable - on and off camera."
BILL

Three Years of Velour

"Even OFF the set I wore velour!"
BILL

WHAT A DIFFERENCE THREE YEARS MAKE

"One thing kids do...
is grow."
ANGELA

SHOOTING FINAL

SHOOTING FINAL

THE JUNK YARD OF SPACE

LOST IN SPACE

SERIES

DECEMBER 28, 1967

AN IRWIN ALLEN PRODUCTION
IN ASSOCIATION WITH
SPACE PRODUCTIONS
AND
TWENTIETH CENTURY-FOX TELEVISION, INC.

FYI *The Junkyard of Space* was the last episode of the series, airing on March 6, 1968; the final day of filming was January 12, 1968.

"I would have to admit it was a bit of a shock. It did seem strange to have no closure after working together for so long. It would be about 22 years before the rest of us would see each other collectively again. By that time, sadly, Guy had passed away."
ANGELA

"I had worked on many television shows and feature films before starting my journey as Will Robinson. I completely understood the reality of an actor's life: booking a job, preparing for the gig, filming the project, and then wrapping it, saying goodbye to the folks you'd just spent anywhere from a few days to several months working closely with and moving on to the next show. That's the nature of the entertainment business.

But, the end of Lost in Space was different.

After three years of working alongside the same group of fine people who became almost like family to me, there was no closure. There was no celebration. There were no hugs, no tears, no kisses, no goodbyes. We were all verbally told that like the previous three seasons and 83 episodes we'd made together, we would be returning to the Jupiter 2 for another season of bizarre adventures after a couple months of hiatus. But for many reasons, probably explained by others better than I could explain here, that was not our destiny.

I can clearly remember the day I heard the news. I had just walked into my family home on Forrester Drive in Cheviot Hills through the front door and I was standing in the stone entryway when my mom called me into the kitchen and told me she'd been on the phone with Howard Rubin, my beloved agent, and he'd informed her that things had changed and Irwin Allen and CBS had decided not to continue with the series and that it was cancelled. It was a real shock to my young brain. It hit me very emotionally and at the peculiar age of 14, not a little kid anymore and not yet a man, my feelings rushed out as tears. I cried. I cried hard. I didn't want it to have ended like that and I was sad and angry about it.

I never saw Guy Williams again. Outside of birthday and Christmas cards, I didn't see June or Marta or Jonathan or Bobby for several years. Mark and I continued to see each other a bit and of course Ange and I were still in school together and growing closer than ever. It was a very sad way to say goodbye to a magnificent experience."

BILL

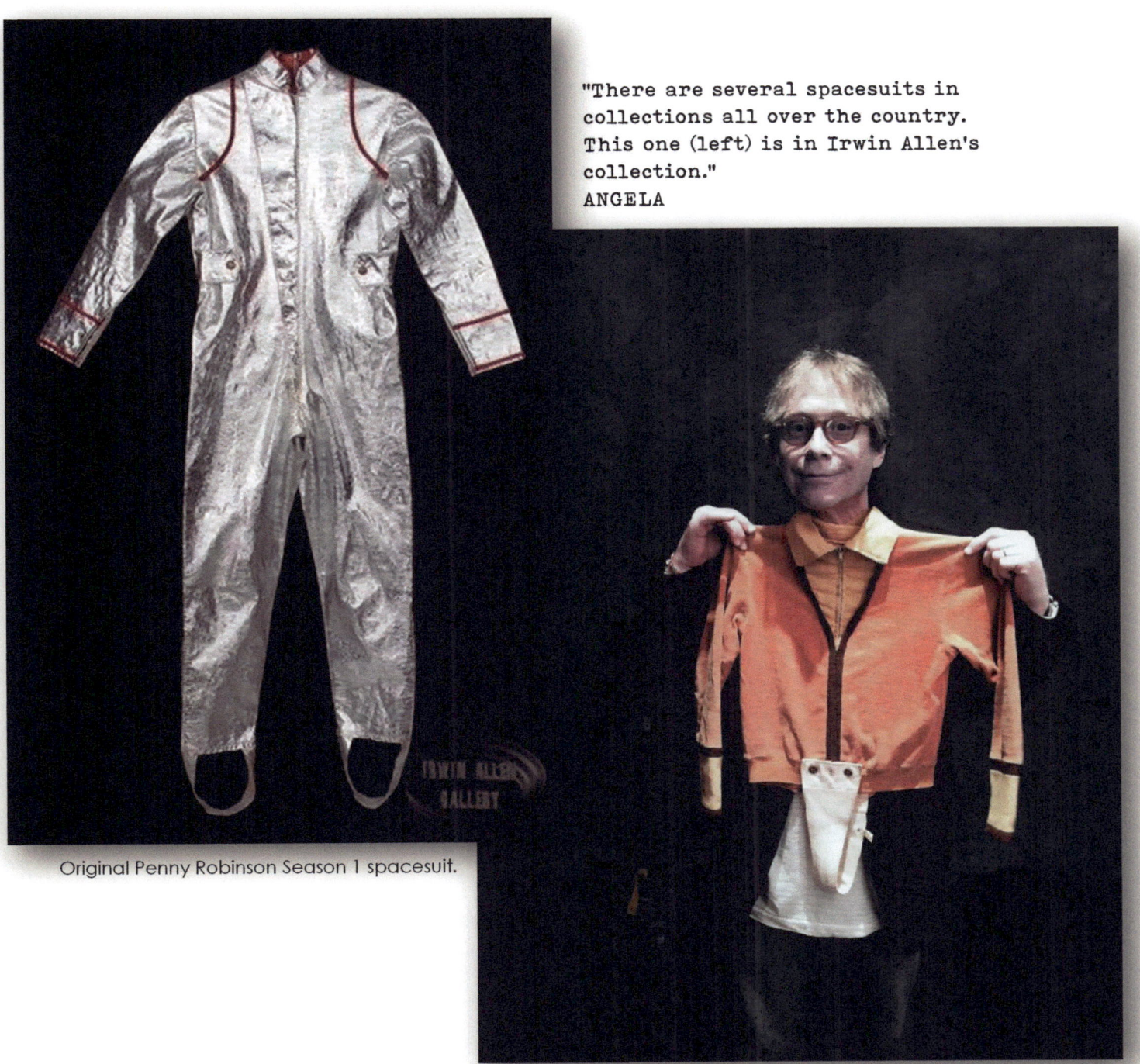

"There are several spacesuits in collections all over the country. This one (left) is in Irwin Allen's collection."
ANGELA

Original Penny Robinson Season 1 spacesuit.

Bill, with his Season 1 costume.

Just Horsing Around

"My father, Charles William Mumy, was a cattle rancher in Bishop, California. Here's a pic of me with him in the 1958 Labor Day parade. He's riding Bonnie and I'm riding Maggie."
BILL

"I've worked with the band America for decades and I am seen here with a horse with no name." BILL

"I started riding horses as a toddler. I even rode a pony in an episode of *The Danny Thomas Show* when I was four. My sister Veronica and I went horseback riding every Saturday. When I was 16 I owned my own horse 'Sunni.' She was skinny and weak when I bought her and over time she became healthy and strong. One day I went out riding and Sunni got very spooked by the windy weather that had kicked up. I decided to head back to the barn as tree branches and debris were blowing all over the place. As we drew near the stable, Sunni took off like she was bolting out of a racetrack gate. She stopped short of the gully that surrounded the stables but I did not and went head over horse landing in a ditch. That was one of those times I was very grateful I walked away with only grit in my eyes."
ANGELA

Photos from Cartwright/Mumy Collections

A Picture's Worth a Thousand Words

Bill Mumy Collection

"Photography has always been a visual journal to me by capturing a moment in time and relaying that information to the viewer. I got totally hooked on analog photography in the 1960s when my parents bought me a Nikon camera for my 15th birthday. I inherited my dad's love of photographs and I learned a lot about images from him. Because he was a technical artist for years, he had an eye for the details. He taught me about that.
Bill shot this picture of me on the beach. I'd never seen it before it was unearthed from who knows where. I'm wearing my boiled wool cape I bought in Salzburg while filming *The Sound of Music*. See the memory this picture brings back? I loved that cape and I wore it for years.
I have hordes of proof sheets and stills that I have yet to sort through. I look forward to the stories and memories they will tell. It used to be that your film had to go to a lab where proof sheets or prints were made. Today, instant gratification! There is no excuse for not exploring this amazing art if you catch the bug, because your phone can be the recorder of your dreams."
ANGELA

Some Things Never Change

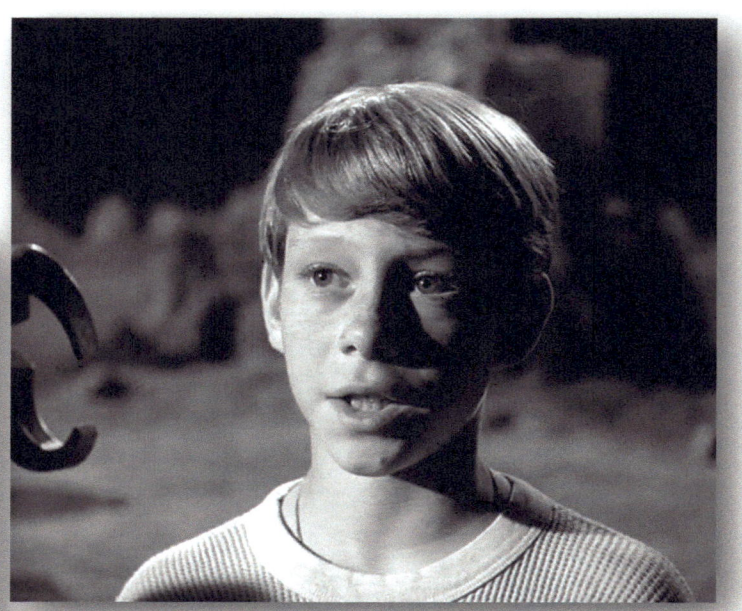

"During the years we filmed *Lost In Space*, I always wore a Saint Christopher medal and my own diving watch. 56 years later, I still wear a Saint Christopher medal and a diving watch. But I very rarely wear any velour these days."
BILL

Bill Mumy Collection

"Social media in the 1970s was the same as it is in the 21st century, only kinder. It was analog with names of teen fan magazines like Flip, Fave, Fab, and Tiger Beat. The articles were filled with embellished stories and sensationalized headlines like 'How to Turn a Tomboy Into A Temptress In 10 Easy Lessons' and 'I Was In Love With A Married Man Until I Met A Monkee.' The married man was supposed to be Mark Goddard, who was more like a crazy uncle than a love interest. The Monkee was Mickey Dolenz, who I had known since his *Circus Boy* days. Showbiz kids were members of a small circle and you often crossed paths.

The magazines would set you up on dates with popular movie, tv, sports, or music peers. In my case it often was Jon Provost, Sajid Kahn, Kurt Russell, Barry Gibb, or Mark Spitz to name a few. We would go on an arranged date to a concert or theme park with a photographer and a publicity person tagging along. The magazine picked up all the expenses and you enjoyed a fun free day. Those pictures would weave a tall tale most of the time. Pictures taken at a party often fabricated relationships, falsely creating who you were dating, inventing drama overnight. I found most of the time it was easier to stay out of the public eye. Though I might revisit those Temptress lessons and remind myself just what they were."

ANGELA

Once a Robinson, Always a Robinson

Photos from Cartwright/Mumy Collections

Beyond Another Irwin Adventure

"I worked for Irwin Allen again after *Lost in Space* in a star-studded epic movie called *Beyond The Poseidon Adventure*. It was a long and difficult shoot where we were cold and soaking wet every day. Mark Harmon and I hit it off right away and we kept each other sane. I so enjoyed working with Michael Caine, who saved our asses more than once. Oh, there are tales of buddy breathing, sharks, fears of drowning, and Irwin banging that damn bucket. The other cast members thought Irwin was crazy, but I was used to it."
ANGELA

Seems Like Old Times

Photos from Cartwright/Mumy Collections

"In 1970, Angela and I were asked to 'entertain the troops' at Port Hueneme naval base in Oxnard, California. So, of course we did. We drove up there and we signed stuff and talked and we sang onstage together, which is one of the only times we ever did that. We sang Paul Simon's *Punky's Dilemma*, a song off of Simon and Garfunkel's *Bookends* album. We were no Sonny and Cher but everyone seemed to enjoy it. I wish there was a recording of that. Or... maybe I don't. But it's a sweet memory in my mind."
BILL

FYI There wouldn't be a full cast reunion until 1990, but there were still opportunities to get some of the 'family' back together.

"Robot, Smith, Will, and Judy spotted on Earth."
BILL

"I always looked forward to December because my annual Christmas Party was always a time to catch up with friends and share the joys of the season."
ANGELA

Photos from Cartwright/Mumy Collections

THE ROBINSONS' FAMILY FEUD

"Playing *Family Feud* for charity was lots of fun. Nerve-wracking, but fun. It's so easy to play these game shows in the comfort of your own home, but under pressure you just hope your brain keeps working. We were able to make some money for June's charity choice as we played against *Gilligan's Island* and *Batman*."
ANGELA

Photos from Angela Cartwright Collection

"Sadly, this was the last time we would see Guy Williams. You never know when that last time will be."
ANGELA

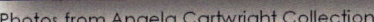

Photos from Angela Cartwright Collection

Something to Talk About...

Bob May, Angela, Marta, Mark, and June in Detroit, *Kelly & Company*, May 5, 1987.

Bill and Angela reunited on the *Pat Sajak Show*, July 21, 1989.

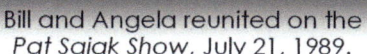

"I was in shock when Pat Sajak took my pristine vintage puzzle and tore open the cellophane on camera. What was he thinking? And then SURPRISE! It's Bill, who I hadn't seen in ages. Usually you get a heads up about surprises, but this really was kept from me and I was truly flummoxed."
ANGELA

"I didn't want to do the *Pat Sajak Show*. They called and pushed really hard to get me to make a surprise appearance while Ange was the featured guest. They promised they would promote the new Marvel graphic novel I had just written, *The Dreamwalker*, and so I reluctantly agreed. When I was announced and walked onstage, Ange and I hadn't seen each other in almost 15 years. It was weird. I sat down next to her and she immediately whispered in my ear, 'What are you DOING here?!' Gadzooks. Then I made a joke that went over poorly and things went from weird to worse. Pat Sajak was a lousy listener and a sour guy. When he tore open Ange's vintage Linda Williams puzzle I could hear every collector in the country gasp in horror."
BILL

Photos from Angela Cartwright Collection

Lost in Pranks

Photo by Eileen Mumy

"Mark and I weren't the only pranksters in the cast. In fact, June definitely wins the award for best practical joke ever and it was on Jonathan, Marta, and I at a 1990 convention at the Shrine Auditorium in Los Angeles where the three of us made a personal appearance together. After a Q & A session onstage, we were lined up to sign autographs and a woman wearing a wig and glasses, who appeared to be very down on her luck, perhaps homeless, stood in line and in a peculiar voice asked to shake hands with Jonathan. When he warily agreed, the woman took his hand in hers enthusiastically and gripped it for quite awhile. Her hands were greasy and clammy and appeared very dirty. The whole episode was quite unsettling. Jonathan grimaced but carried on. As soon as the autograph session was over, we discovered it was June in disguise with Vaseline on her hands! She had us all totally fooled! That prank took a lot of planning and work from her. It was brilliant and without any shadow of a doubt, it was definitely Jonathan's very favorite all-time memory of June. He roared every time he told the story and they became closer than ever after that. For awhile anyway."
BILL

Bill Mumy Collection

"*The Invaders*, starring Roy Thinnes, was a popular series from 1967 to 1968. It was a show about an alien nation from a dying planet invading the earth. You could tell they were the aliens because of their expressionless face and deformed little finger that bent at an unnatural angle. One day we were filming what we called a 'raking 6,' a shot where we stood as a group lined up watching a scene off camera. June was a huge fan of *The Invaders* and with a twinkle in her eye directed us to stand motionless holding our pinky fingers 'Invaders' style while the camera rolled. The best part... nobody ever knew, but us. Unfortunately I can't remember what episode it was in... maybe you can!"
ANGELA

Reunited at Last - Boston 1990

"The 1990 *Lost in Space* Boston reunion show was a blast. Kevin Burns had asked me to reach out and 'feel' how the rest of the cast would react to doing it while it was still in the planning stages. I did as he asked and it was 100% positive in every way. There were some moments where we indeed held our breath, but in the end it all worked out perfectly. Before we were all introduced to the audience, we were huddled together in a small tent-like structure in the convention center where Jonathan and June both gave excellent pep talks. It was like being on a professional sports team about to play a big game. I loved it. I only wish Guy Williams had lived long enough to have been a part of that. He would have truly appreciated the joy and love the fans felt for the series."
BILL

Candid photos by Tom McLaren

...AND BOSTON AGAIN IN 1995

"Don't mind me...just smelling your hair."
BILL

Candid photos by Tom McLaren

"Five years later there was another big event reuniting the Robinsons once again. These events were the closest I've ever felt to being a rock star. Tons of screaming fans. None of us could believe it! The first Boston reunion in 1990 was indeed incredible with some 80,000 people who turned out for the event. I don't think any of us realized the emotional impact this show had on so many and the outpouring of love and appreciation was undeniable."
ANGELA

Bill Mumy Collection

THE FANTASY WORLDS OF IRWIN ALLEN™

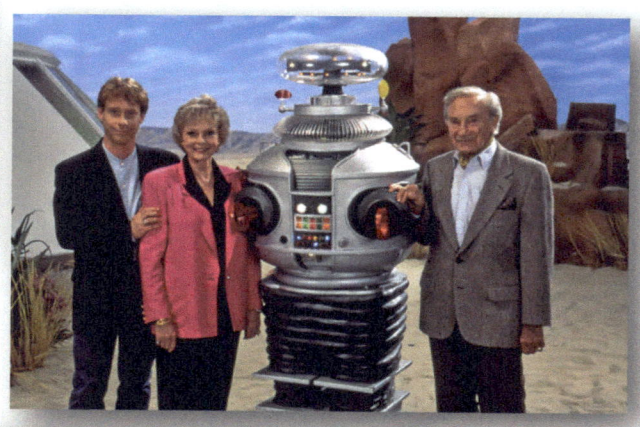

"Co-hosting *The Fantasy Worlds of Irwin Allen* was a blast. Kevin Burns wrote, produced, and directed a really cool special that saluted Irwin's huge imagination and amazing accomplishments."
BILL

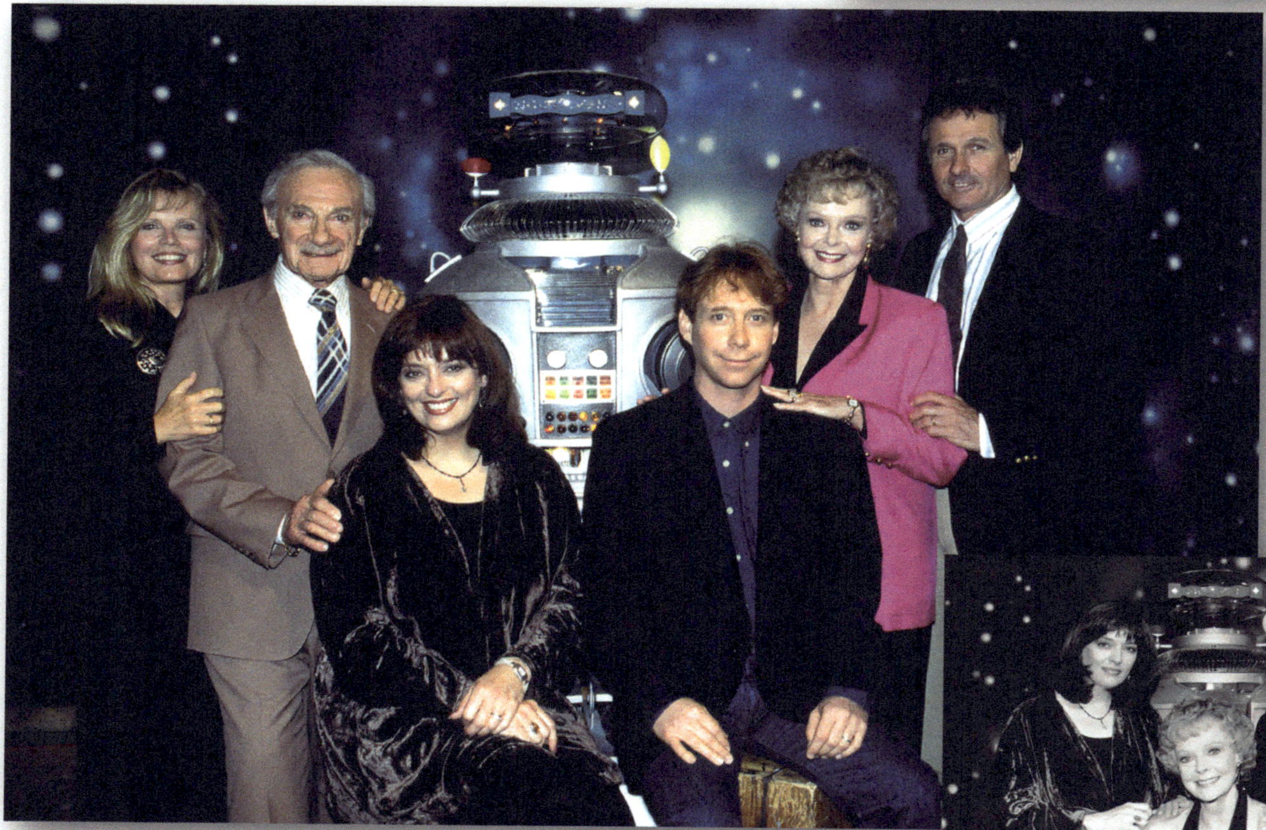

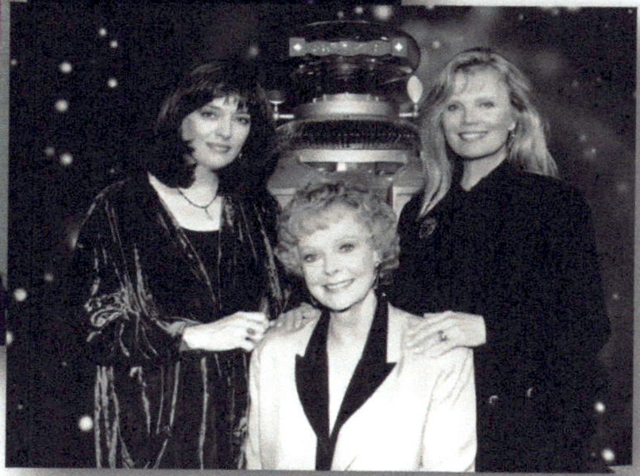

"I wrote both bits where Jonathan, Bobby, and I had our 'moment' in front of the Jupiter 2. When I first walked onto the stage that morning it felt great to be on the replicated Jupiter 2 set... but Kevin noticed that I was somehow a bit 'off' in my reaction. He asked what I was feeling and I confessed to him that I felt it all seemed somehow smaller to me. He wisely assured me this was because I had grown since the last time I had been on that exact scale set! He was right."
BILL

FOXSTAR PRODUCTIONS and EMMETT STREET FILMS announce the Los Angeles premiere of
"LOST IN SPACE FOREVER"
Sunday, November 28, 1998
3:00 p.m. PST

To be broadcast on KTTV-Fox 11 —and in syndication nationwide— through December 10, 1998

Eileen, Seth, and Liliana Mumy on the set with Bill.

FYI Like father, like son... Seth Mumy visited the set of *Lost in Space Forever* in a custom-made Robinson flight suit.

Candid Photos from Bill Mumy Collection

Blast Off Day 1997

> **FYI** In 1997 the series was honored by the Museum of Television and Radio with a full cast appearance including Bob May and Dick Tufeld. The event featured a panel and screening.

Museum of Television and Radio panel discussion with Steve Bell.
Photo by Eileen Mumy

"You can see from the wine glasses everyone had a drink or two... or five." ANGELA

"Blast Off Day was beyond crazy. It was flattering to be honored at the Museum of Television and Radio in Beverly Hills. Steve Bell, who ran it, had worked closely with Kevin Burns at Fox and they certainly hosted a very classy event.
BUT... it was quite nearly a huge train wreck. It was a very warm evening and we had been posing for photographs in the lobby together alongside a Robot for several hours and the caterers had never-ending trays of champagne that we all enjoyed. Too much, perhaps.
The truth is we all got very buzzed before going onstage for a panel of questions and answers together. Mark was blitzed and blithered on about being dead. Jonathan was blitzed and came very close to crossing some lines of behavior and I was blitzed and did my best to stop him from crossing those lines. June seemed to delight in the chaos and she lit the fuse to the biggest bomb of the night. June had convinced the powers that be to play the unaired pilot *No Place To Hide*. The theater was darkened and they started running it and Jonathan became incensed. And I don't blame him. He's not IN the unaired pilot. So, Kevin Burns rushed up to the projection booth and the screening stopped and they switched to *The Reluctant Stowaway*, the first episode of the series.
The evening ended nicely and everyone calmed down and sobered up. But for a little while there... danger! danger! we were headed for a crash landing!"
BILL

Left to right: Heather Graham, Jack Johnson, Marta, Angela, Lacey Chabert.

My continuity pic.

Photos from Angela Cartwright Collection

Marta and me in our reporter wardrobe.

"When it was announced that New Line would make a *Lost In Space* movie, I realized it was time to pass the baton to a new Penny. I was asked if I would do a cameo with Marta as reporters and I was happy to do that as a nod to our loyal *Lost In Space* followers and a cool trip to my homeland in the United Kingdom. I'll never understand why they didn't cast Bill, the original Will, as the grownup Will in that movie. It all made no sense whatsoever, but hey, that's showbiz."
ANGELA

Angela and Marta at the Los Angeles premiere.

Photos from Cartwright/Mumy Collections

Bill, Jack Johnson, and Jonathan at the NY premiere.

"I met with Stephen Hopkins and Akiva Goldsman as the project was being prepped. They were nice. They had read all my *Lost in Space* comic books and had very positive things to say about them. I read the script. I told them that if business details could be worked out regarding my obligations to *Babylon 5*, I would play the role of the older Will Robinson. New Line ultimately decided they did not want to cast me in that part. They only wanted me to do a cameo. I said 'No Thank You.' I have zero regrets about that. When the film was being readied for release, New Line again aggressively pursued Jonathan and me to come onboard somehow. They ended up flying us to New York, first class, putting us up in lovely suites in a fabulous hotel and paying us each a lot of money to go to the premiere and walk the red carpet and chat with the press.

It was a chilly rainy night. Jonathan and I had dinner together in the hotel and then got into the limousine and were driven to the theater. We walked and waved and were seated together and we watched the film.

It's the one and only time I've watched it.

When it was over, we again were paraded down the red carpet and the reporters from various news shows, etc. were thrusting their cameras and mics in our faces. 'Jonathan Harris and Bill Mumy... the original Dr. Smith and Will Robinson! What did you think of the movie?!?' I answered honestly 'I thought the ship looked cool.' Jonathan blew my mind. He was so honest and so great. His reply?: 'It was so loud! It gave me a terrible headache. Ohhh, the pain.'"
BILL

TV Guide Photo Shoot

"The TV Guide shoot reunited us all again for an article on the New Line *Lost In Space* movie. The studio reproduced many of the classic collectibles to create some buzz for the movie. But I don't think it helped make the movie more popular."
ANGELA

"As always, it was nice to be together with everyone for this TV Guide photo shoot. There was quite a lot of Lost In Space energy around back then for the classic cast as well as the New Line feature. Ange and I drove down to Culver City together for the shoot and then went out afterwards for a cocktail and toasted Debbie the Bloop. Indeed!"
BILL

Return to Earth Celebration

The Jeneraters on stage:
Bill, Miguel Ferrer, Tom Hebenstreit.

"The *Return To Earth Celebration* produced by Kevin Burns in 1998, was the first and only convention dedicated wholly to *Lost In Space*. We did panels and a bunch of interviews but the highlight was when Bill rocked it on stage."
ANGELA

Photos by Eileen Mumy

You and a Guest are cordially invited
to join Foxstar Productions
and
Everyday Productions
in Celebrating Television's Original
Lost in Space

Please join Series Cast Members,
Mrs. Irwin Allen and Special Surprise Guests
For the
Lost in Space
"Return to Earth Celebration"

Friday, April 3rd
4-7pm
Hollywood Entertainment Museum
7021 Hollywood Boulevard
Hollywood, CA 90028

RSVP 310 369-4546

celebrating THE FANTASY WORLDS OF IRWIN ALLEN

Photos from Tom McLaren Collection

Bill photobombing Angela with Tom McLaren and Marta.

Lost in Space
Staged Radio Drama
Hollywood, April 1998

> "I wrote the staged radio play for the Hollywood *Return to Earth Celebration* convention with tongue firmly in cheek as a special bonus treat for the fans to hear the classic cast of *Lost in Space* once again in character, acknowledging the new *Lost in Space* feature film and Jonathan's and my *Twilight Zone* alumni status thinking it would be a lot of fun. I hadn't read it in over 20 years when I rediscovered it for this expanded edition. I think it's a bummer we didn't do it, but that's showbiz."
> BILL

Written By Bill Mumy
© 1998
All Rights Reserved

ROBOT Warning! Warning!

SMITH Silence, you cantankerous clump, can't your senile sensors see that I'm trying to take a nap?

WILL What is it, robot?

ROBOT There is an unknown spacecraft approaching. My sensors compute it is heading directly for us.

WILL Send them a message. Tell them we need repairs. Maybe they can help us!

ROBOT Communication with this ship is not possible Will Robinson. I have scanned all known frequencies and have not been able to get through to them.

SMITH When at first you don't succeed, try, try again you metal moron! Continue scanning! Perhaps they can help us leave this miserable world and return to glorious earth!

DON Until we know what we're facing, let's not take any chance. Give me a hand with the forcefield Will.

MAUREEN Penny, Judy, you'd better get up here. And bring the laser guns with you.

JUDY What's going on, mother?

PENNY Are we under attack?

MAUREEN We don't know. Probably not. But it's better to play it safe.

PENNY We'll be right up.

SMITH Put yourself to good use, ninny. Get outside and scan the area. Use your sensors to identify what you have so far failed to.

ROBOT 'Tis a far better thing that I...

SMITH Spare us the dramatics you bumbling bubble headed boob! Go!

ROBOT Affirmative.

PENNY Here are the lasers. I sure hope we won't have to use them.

JUDY Have you determined what's out there?

MAUREEN Not yet. But look! Outside! The light... it's changing!

DON The force field's activated. Whatever it is that's headed our way, it won't be able to breach the perimeter of the field.

WILL Something feels wrong here. I don't like it...

PENNY Here comes the robot. Maybe he's computed what we're facing.

ROBOT It does not compute. It does not compute. It does not compute.

SMITH I knew it. He's useless to us. As usual.

WILL Something's scrambled his sensor banks, Dr. Smith! This is serious.

JUDY Look!

MAUREEN Oh my god!

PENNY What is that?!? I can't make it out!

DON It's coming through the force field!! Like it's walking right through paper!

SMITH We're doomed. Doomed I tell you!

WILL It's getting so dark... I can't see clearly. But ... woah! It looks kinda like...

ROBOT My sensors indicate there are seven humanoid beings and one sentient machine.

JUDY I can see them!

PENNY They look like... they look like us!

WILL Like we used to look. A long time ago.

SMITH Speak for yourself. I'm much handsomer than any of them.

DON They're pointing something at us!

MAUREEN Robot, can you compute what it is?

ROBOT It is danger! Danger, Will Robinson!

PENNY But what exactly is it, robot?

ROBOT It is state of the art computer graphic images! It is an eighty million dollar budget!

JUDY It's getting darker!

WILL I feel really strange...

PENNY Me too!

SMITH Oh the pain, the pain!

DON What's happening to us?!

MAUREEN Who are they?! What are they doing?!

ROBOT My sensors indicate that they are us!

MAUREEN But... that can't be!

SMITH For once I agree with you madam, there is only one Dr. Zachary Smith!

DON Yeah, one too many!

SMITH Spare me your witty verbalisms, Major. William! What's happening? Oh dear, oh dear... I feel so strange.

WILL Me too, like... I'm fading away...

ROBOT We are being transported to another dimension!

PENNY What?!

DON What?

ROBOT The fifth dimension!

WILL How is that possible?!

ROBOT We are being displaced to a shadowy tip of reality!

MAUREEN Don't ask me how I know, but... don't be afraid! It's going to be alright.

SMITH Speak for yourself madam. I prefer reality as I know it!

JUDY Ooohhhh... it's coming from their robot! It's sending us away!

MAUREEN At least we're all together!

WILL Robot, did you say the fifth dimension?!

ROBOT Affirmative Will Robinson. We are being displaced to a dimension not only of sight and sound, but of mind.

SMITH Still you continue to babble, booby?! Help me! Save me! I'm too young and handsome to be dimensionally displaced!

PENNY Look! The Jupiter 2's disappearing!

ROBOT We are now entering the middle ground between light and shadow, between science and superstition.

WILL You're right mom! I can feel it too! It's gonna be okay! We're going to a... a better place!

ROBOT We are being transported to a place that lies between the pit of man's fears and the summit of his knowledge!

SMITH You know William, I have the strangest feeling that I've been here before! A long, long time ago!

WILL Yeah. Me too, Dr. Smith!

MAUREEN Look! Up ahead!

JUDY What is it?

DON It's a signpost!

PENNY What's it say?!

ROBOT It says... we have now entered... the *Twilight Zone*!

WILL Cool.

THE END

ONCE A COMIC GEEK...

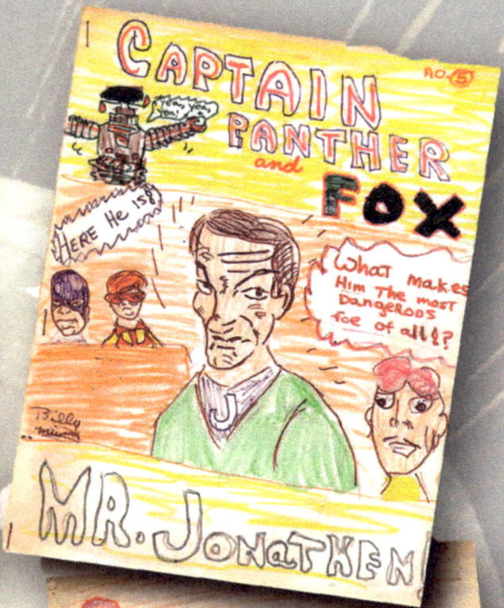

Bill Mumy Collection

"When I wasn't filming, going to school, at lunch, or goofing around in general, I was huddled on the stage writing and drawing superhero comic books that were based on the cast. The first one I made featured Guy and June. In reality, Guy was obsessed with his hair. He was constantly checking it before the camera rolled, so I nicknamed him The Comb and created a superhero who uses various types of combs as weapons. The Comb (and his crime-busting beauty Cara Mia) was a one issue special edition Mumy comic. Then I did a whole series starring Mark and me as *Captain Panther and Fox*. The Comb and Cara Mia returned in a few of those stories. All of the villains were based on various *Lost in Space* cast and crew members. The comic books are crude, sloppy, and very silly, but I had fun making them. In the 1990s I wrote the *Lost in Space* comic book for real. I have always had a lot of restless creative energy."
BILL

Background illustration by Michal Dutkiewicz

THAN A FEW CRASH LANDINGS, PICKING UP, BEING REPAIRED WITH AND ASSIMILATING ALIEN TECHNOLOGY GATHERED ALONG YOUR VOYAGE FROM MANY WORLDS FAR MORE ADVANCED THAN EARTH...

Dr. MAUREEN ROBINSON

"I wrote the *Lost in Space* comic book series published by Innovation Comics for two years, 1991-1993. The books were successful and critically very well-received. I really enjoyed writing those stories and revisiting characters I honestly felt I knew better than almost anyone else. I was fortunate to work with many talented artists telling those tales. *Voyage to the Bottom of the Soul* became a 360 page ambitious *Lost in Space* graphic novel that really moved the arc of the classic characters in a big way. I felt real good about that one. Stan Lee generously wrote the foreword to it. It's been out-of-print for quite awhile now, and I'm hoping to republish it soon."
BILL

Bill Mumy Collection

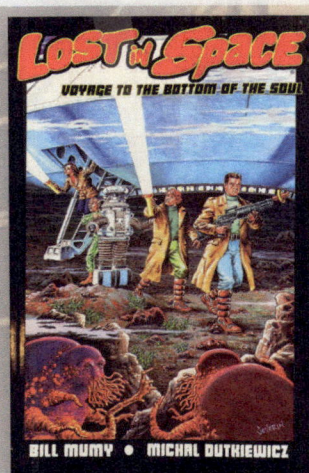

OCTOBER 16, 1997. REMEMBER THE DAY. SHORTLY AFTER BLAST OFF FOR YOUR TARGET, ALPHA CENTAURI, YOUR ENVIRONMENTAL ROBOT, B-9, WHO

"In the mid-1980s I co-wrote three issues of the classic *Star Trek* comic book for DC Comics and I was fortunate to work with Jerome K. Moore on those issues. It was a slightly veiled 'Trek meets Lost In Space' saga. When writing the *Lost In Space* Innovation comic books in the early 1990s, Jerome again supplied some fabulous art, including this piece below."
BILL

Artwork by George Broderick Jr.

Artwork by Jerome K. Moore and Jason Palmer

"I've never been a huge follower of comic books (unlike someone else I know), but I have to admit I have enjoyed the imagination in the illustrations and I have always loved my voluptuous figure and this cover with *The Diary of Penny Robinson*. Magical."
ANGELA

The Family That Works Together...

Pioneers of Television.

On the Edge of Black and White.

FYI In 2000, Jonathan and Bill were teamed up and back in the studio together again to guest star in two episodes of Disney's *Buzz Lightyear of Star Command*.

Photos from Cartwright/Mumy Collections

"June and I did an episode of *Ren and Stimpy* together which was really cool, and June also guest starred in an episode of *Babylon 5*. Our characters didn't have any scenes together, but we were planning on doing a 'walk down the hallway' shot where we passed each other and paused to give 'a look' and then walk on... however that was the week of the big 1994 earthquake, and as it turned out, with aftershocks and stress, there was no extra time for frivolity."
BILL

Angela and Bill narrated the *Ancient Aliens* audiobook.

FYI Angela, Bill, Marta, and Jonathan worked on the 2009 animated short *The Bolt Who Screwed Christmas*, supplying voices to various characters in this holiday project that turned out to be Jonathan's final voiceover job (released several years after his passing).

OVERLOAD — OH, THE PAIN...

"While working on the science fiction series *Babylon 5* from 1993 thru 1998 playing the alien Lennier, I became close friends with Tony Dow, the legendary child actor best known for his iconic role as Wally in *Leave it to Beaver*. Tony and I had met at events over the decades, but we never really knew each other until he became a director on B5. He's a truly super great guy.

As a series regular, I would receive first drafts of upcoming scripts a few weeks in advance and sometimes Joe Straczynski, the series creator, writer, and executive producer, would ask me for some casting suggestions. More than once, I suggested Billy Gray for a guest appearance. Billy, in my opinion, was one of the very best young actors of all time. His performances in *The Day the Earth Stood Still*, an *Adventures of Superman* episode and most iconically his many seasons as Bud Anderson on *Father Knows Best* made big impressions on me. Billy was famously busted for a small amount of marijuana back in the early 1960s and that arrest basically ended his acting career. So, more than a few times, I'd say to Joe, 'It would be so cool to have Billy Gray play this part!'

Well, Joe actually brought Billy in at least once, but things didn't work out. One day at the studio, Tony heard me singing Billy's praises to Joe and he asked me if I knew Billy. I told him I'd never met him, but I was a big fan. 'He's my neighbor and a close friend... you wanna meet him?' I did indeed. So, my wife Eileen and I had dinner out at Tony's fabulous home in Topanga Canyon with Billy and we ended up playing ping-pong all night and we all got along great. We continued to hang out and have ping-pong tournaments. Billy ALWAYS won.

That is what inspired me to create *Overload*. I thought I could be the guy to relaunch Billy Gray's acting career and along the way I would spearhead a project that showcased the talents of others who grew up as child stars. I asked Billy if he'd be into returning to acting should the opportunity present itself and he said, 'why, sure.'

Peter David was my writing partner in those days. He and I created and wrote *Space Cases* together. We came up with a script that was similar (we felt) to a *Twilight Zone* vibe. *Overload* was a space drama that dealt with survival and spirituality and man's hubris in the face of certain doom. The characters were created for specific actors... Billy Gray, Johnny Crawford, Tony Dow, Veronica Cartwright, Angela Cartwright, Don Grady, George Takei, and myself along with a voiceover character for Melissa Gilbert. Tony would direct it. He and I would produce it and Don Grady would compose the score. The script was sold to Galaxy Pictures and a deal was made. It was a fair deal for everyone. Sets were built. The crew was hired. Wardrobe, special effects shots, miniatures, CGI, etc. all went into production. Veronica was committed to another project at the time and Claudia Christian from *Babylon 5* replaced her in *Overload*.

We filmed for a week and all was going great. Then, all went not great. Galaxy ran into trouble and out of money and production ended. We scraped together an impressive trailer from what had been shot to pitch to backers, but Galaxy went bankrupt and basically disappeared into the ether. But because they had bought and paid for the script and the existing footage, we couldn't claim it and shop it around to find a new home to complete it. The *Overload* trailer can be seen if you look hard enough for it. I think it was going to be great had we completed it. But that wasn't meant to be. Showbiz. Shit like that happens more than you'd believe."
BILL

Photo from Bill Mumy Collection

Overload - A Galaxy Pictures Production in association with Stargate Films. The cast clockwise from left: Angela Cartwright, George Takei, Tony Dow, Don Grady, Claudia Christian, Billy Gray, Johnny Crawford, and Bill Mumy.

Clockwise: Veronica Cartwright, Billy Gray, Johnny Crawford, Bill, Angela, Don Grady, and Tony Dow.

Photos from Cartwright/Mumy Collections

Sights and Sounds

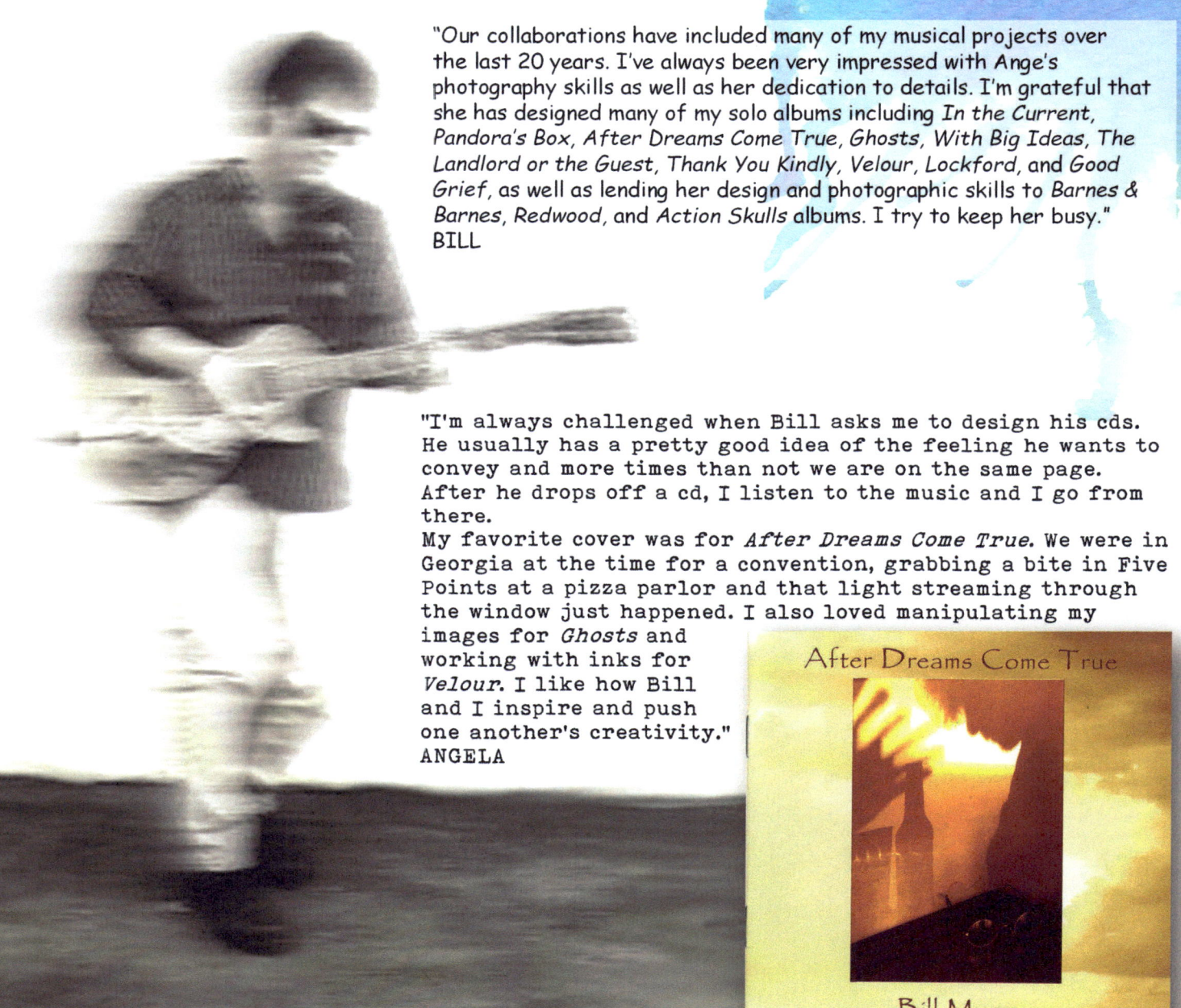

"Our collaborations have included many of my musical projects over the last 20 years. I've always been very impressed with Ange's photography skills as well as her dedication to details. I'm grateful that she has designed many of my solo albums including *In the Current*, *Pandora's Box*, *After Dreams Come True*, *Ghosts*, *With Big Ideas*, *The Landlord or the Guest*, *Thank You Kindly*, *Velour*, *Lockford*, and *Good Grief*, as well as lending her design and photographic skills to *Barnes & Barnes*, *Redwood*, and *Action Skulls* albums. I try to keep her busy."
BILL

"I'm always challenged when Bill asks me to design his cds. He usually has a pretty good idea of the feeling he wants to convey and more times than not we are on the same page. After he drops off a cd, I listen to the music and I go from there.
My favorite cover was for *After Dreams Come True*. We were in Georgia at the time for a convention, grabbing a bite in Five Points at a pizza parlor and that light streaming through the window just happened. I also loved manipulating my images for *Ghosts* and working with inks for *Velour*. I like how Bill and I inspire and push one another's creativity."
ANGELA

A Visit to NASA

Photos from Angela Cartwright Collection

"Show business is not always glamourous and a barrel of laughs. It is hard work with disciplined hours and a great responsibility to bring to the set whenever you perform. But there are sometimes perks that also come your way and our visit to NASA and the Kennedy Space Center was one of those unforgettable highlights. On Monday, March 5, 2001, Bill and his son Seth, Marta Kristen, my son Jesse, and I were given a grand tour of the Kennedy Space Center. The *Endeavour* was being constructed for its future missions in space. It was an up-close and personal tour of awesomeness.

From the runway we saw the arrival of the space shuttle Atlantis riding piggyback on a 747 and were given a crash course inside an actual shuttle trainer jet by astronaut Charlie Justiz. We also chatted with multiple technicians in the Mission Control area, almost all of whom were huge *Lost In Space* fans. We got a good look inside *Discovery* as it was being prepared for its liftoff a couple of days later. We gathered on the launch pad and looked up as the *Discovery* stood boldly ready for its trip into the heavens. I was overwhelmed by the enormity and thrill of it all. The highlight, however, was seeing the actual launch of *Discovery* on March 8, 2001. That is something I will never forget.

Rising at 4:00 am and driving to Cape Canaveral I was filled with anticipation. Even the ofttimes recalcitrant Bill, who had complained about rising in the early hours, admitted the experience was well worth the lost sleep. In the chilly early morning air we huddled in the grandstands enveloped in positive energy, holding our breath as we silently prayed for a safe and successful launch. We watched as a gigantic clock counted down the seconds and then the earth rumbled beneath our feet and a blast of hot air blew over us as the *Discovery* took off into the beyond. It was a perfect launch, lifting off on schedule at 6:45 am into a stunning sunrise.

After the launch we were invited to join everyone at Mission Control for their traditional celebratory 'beans and cornbread' meal. (It was a bit tough on our stomachs at the crack of dawn, but everyone there had been up all night.) The area was filled with astronauts, their families, military personnel, such as General Colin Powell, and many employees. Those we met at NASA shared with us their excitement about what they were accomplishing. We were told more than once how *Lost In Space* had fed their dreams as children and inspired them to go into the space program as adults.

I continued to be amazed at the impact our show had on people and how it had captured their imaginations. I know how very privileged we were to have enjoyed such an intimate tour. Many thanks to Astronaut Charlie Justiz, Louie Garcia, and all who made this happen."

ANGELA

"I'm so glad our sons Seth and Jesse were able to share this amazing moment in history with us as we watched the launch and were allowed to see inside the *Endeavour* and look around thinking 'How could it possibly hold seven astronauts at a time?' The *Endeavor* went on to successfully complete 25 missions. What an honor when we were asked to 'sign the wall' outside the *Endeavor's* hatch. The wall was filled with a multitude of famous names and my signature is right below Margaret Thatcher."

ANGELA

Photos from Cartwright/Mumy Collections

Guy Williams Hollywood Walk of Fame Ceremony

FYI Guy passed away from a brain aneurysm in Argentina in 1989 at the age of 65.

Guy's real family (kneeling) and his space family (standing).

Photo by Jesse Gullion

Standing L-R: Bob May, Bill, Angela, Guy Williams Jr,, Marta Kristen, Francine York. Seated L-R: Dick Tufeld, Jonathan Harris, Sheila Allen.

"On August 2, 2001, we all gathered on the Hollywood Walk of Fame while Guy Williams posthumously received his star. In addition to the *Lost In Space* cast, there were several members from *Zorro* and a few people that had worked with Guy in movies. The dedication began with Guy's son Steve Catalano (Guy Williams, Jr.) and his daughter Toni. Johnny Grant made the presentation and then we all celebrated over a meal at the Roosevelt Hotel. I sure wish Guy could have been there."
ANGELA

"I think he was there."
BILL

Photos by Jesse Gullion

Back on the Fox lot

"For most of the 1990s when Kevin Burns worked on the Fox lot, he found multiple reasons to reunite the *Lost in Space* group. Sometimes it was to promote the series in syndication, or to include a vintage *Lost In Space* gag in a modern day Fox production, but mostly it was to socialize. After years of disconnection, it was Kevin's passion for the show and his generosity that really brought us all back together and re-bonded us as family."
BILL

Photos from Cartwright/Mumy Collections

"After the show ended I looked forward to the lunches we would have on the 20th Century Fox lot with the whole cast. We would sit in the Shirley Temple room while Jonathan ordered crispy onion rings and a Cobb salad with extra blue cheese dressing. We would settle in with our lunch to hear him tell the same stories every time we got together. We never minded. We laughed and reflected on those times we spent together. Jonathan was a consummate storyteller and I adored him."
ANGELA

Photos from Cartwright/Mumy Collections

"This is the last photograph taken of the luncheon group, Bill and me with Jonathan, Marta, June, Bob May, Sheila Allen, and Dick Tufeld."
ANGELA

"Kevin Burns absolutely loved hosting *Lost in Space* parties. He enjoyed bringing us all back together to the Fox lot where we spent so many happy times filming the classic series. Kevin was very much into details. For Jonathan's 101st birthday party, he had a cake and card duplicated to match ones from 1967 and he flew Mark in from Boston (first class), as a Special Surprise Guest Star."
BILL

Kevin Burns, Eileen Mumy, Mary & Tom McLaren, Marta, Bill, Angela, and Steve Gullion.

"For Kevin's private parties on the Fox lot we either dined in the Shirley Temple Room or in Rupert Murdoch's private dining suite. Ruth's Chris Steak House and Marino Ristorante were two of Kevin's other favorite haunts. He always invited our spouses and one time brought this bust of Jonathan to sit at the head of the table. Kinda weird but we had a good laugh over it and whenever we got together after that, the bust of Jonathan was always there and a splendid time was had by all." ANGELA

Photos from Mumy/McLaren Colections

Tom McLaren, Marta, and Angela.

"On April 6, 2017, I was on the 20th Century Fox lot with Tom McLaren doing a book signing for the paperback edition of our book *Styling The Stars: Lost Treasures from the Twentieth Century Fox Archive*. The book was a collection of continuity and behind the scenes photographs from all the great stars who had made movies at Fox over the last 90 years.

Tom and I had spent two years in the archives at the studio and people working on the lot were anxious to see the history of the continuity shots we had uncovered. Marta dropped by and I stopped in the Fox lot cafe where, lo and behold, this iconic picture of Debbie the Bloop, Bill, and I graces the walls. It's right up there with having a sandwich named after you."

ANGELA

Candid photos from Tom McLaren

Morning Show Laughs

Photos from Cartwright/Mumy Collections

"Celebrating our 50th Anniversary on a morning show led us to remember some funny memories while filming *Lost In Space*."
ANGELA

Lisa Breckenridge and Steve Edwards with June, Angela, Bill, and Marta on Good Day LA, January 20, 2015.

50th Anniversary Blu-Ray Release & The Epilogue

"On March 4, 2015, to celebrate the 50th anniversary, the Jupiter 2 and her crew finally made it back to Earth. 20th Century Fox Home Entertainment agreed to release the entire Lost In Space series, meticulously remastered on blu-ray. The release date was set for September 15, 2015. The studio requested as much bonus material as could be included. Kevin Burns enlisted me as a partner to co-produce the bonus bits and collectively we decided to include Lost in Space: The Epilogue (the often rumored never seen 1980 script I co-wrote with Paul Gordon and Brian Greer resolving the fate of the original series).

To pull it off, after I gave it a serious re-write, Kevin and I produced an ambitious eight camera 'table read' that included Ange, Mark, Marta, and me reprising our original roles along with Guy Williams, Jr. as John Robinson, Veronica Cartwright as Maureen Robinson, Toni Williams, Michael Vahanian, Robert Clotworthy, and Kevin himself as Dr. Smith. When we got into editing, we grew even bolder and included newly created special effects, plus some classic Lost in Space score and outtakes from the original series. For me, it was a satisfying closure to a beloved project after more than 50 years."
BILL

"For the four of us it was a very emotional and satisfying experience. We had slipped back into the characters of Will, Penny, Don, and Judy like we'd never stopped and we finally had closure as the Robinsons returned to Earth. I loved every minute of it, what a memory."
ANGELA

Photos from Angela Cartwright Collection

Tom McLaren Collection

Bill, Veronica Cartwright, Guy Williams, Jr., and Robert Clotworthy, the narrator of *The Epilogue*.

"We all had a blast recording the commentary for the *Lost In Space* blu-ray. We watched episodes of the series and made unrehearsed comments. We had plenty of laughs as the memories flowed. If you love the show, its worth listening to for a few giggles."
ANGELA

Photos from Angela Cartwright Collection

Far Out Time at Comic-Con

"I have a long association with the San Diego Comic-Con going back to the early 1970s. I've attended many of them over the decades. I've gone as a fan/collector, as an invited guest because of my sci-fi acting work, as a comic book writer, and as a musician.
The band Seduction Of The Innocent, comprised of professional comic book talent, was created at Comic-Con and we played many years of parties there. In 2015, Comic-Con hosted the Lost In Space cast to honor the 50th Anniversary. They treated us great. We did panels, signings, radio, tv, and press promotion. The Con surprised me by awarding me a lifetime achievement Inkpot Award. It was a real good weekend."
BILL

Photos from Cartwright/Mumy/McLaren Collections

"Comic-Con is a huge public relations studio event with over 150,000 attendees. We were very proud for *Lost In Space* to be included alongside major fanboy classics like *Deadpool*, *Star Wars-the Force Awakens* and *The Walking Dead* to celebrate our 50th Anniversary. I was just relieved we had someone directing us to where we needed to go next. The convention was so huge that, believe me if we hadn't, we really would have gotten lost in space."
ANGELA

Photos from Bill Mumy Collection

"During our several days at the San Diego Comic-Con in 2015, we did more publicity promoting the series than ever. Several hours in a press room shifting from table to table talking with various reporters from various magazines, newspapers, and podcasts from all over the world took up one morning while the friendly folks from Fox led us from one to the other. We were also taken to several radio stations for live interviews and photo ops. One of the highlights of that weekend was an appearance on a very impressive yacht in the Marina. TV Guide was hosting a party and conducting on-camera interviews as well as still photo sessions. The still photographers worked hard to get us to do stupid poses and act silly, but if memory serves me well, I managed to avoid making a fool of myself for once. They served gourmet food as well as junk food and the booze was definitely flowing freely. We cruised around the harbor with the wind whipping and the sea gulls squawking in the salty air and enjoyed the fact that 50 years on, people were still getting a kick out of Lost in Space. There was some cool swag bags given out when we got off the yacht as I recall, but I missed getting one of those."
BILL

Photos from Bill Mumy Collection

Artwork by Bob Bentovoy

50th Anniversary poster the cast signed at Comic-Con to celebrate the blu-ray release.

319

A Novel Purpose Quest

Photos from Cartwright/Mumy Collection

"Some things happen very quickly, and others take quite a long time. Our novel is a perfect example of a project that fits both those statements. One thing I know for sure... it was meant to be. My kids were grown, I was self-reflecting, searching, and hungering for a purpose.

Bill happened upon the same path one day, I'm not sure exactly how. I think it was over a couple of tacos and a few margaritas, but that tiny speck of imagination blossomed, and our quirky novel was born. A story created before the age of Zoom, by volleying paragraphs and chapters between each other over the phone and in person.

In addition, this novel came to life with artwork and music. The art spilled out of me as I painted each character in 23 paintings and the same happened for Bill who wrote a soundtrack with 27 instrumentals which lyrically colored the adventure. It was certainly a journey I'm proud of and a purpose quest of our own. We'll be re-releasing it soon with a new title: *Stolen Imaginations*.

We all have a purpose. Find yours."

ANGELA

Angela painting one of the illustrations for the novel.

Candid photos from Cartwright/Mumy Collection

Bill working on the soundtrack for the novel.

"Yes, we started writing *Stolen Imaginations* quite a while ago..."
BILL

Lost in Art

'To Be Continued...'
Bill Mumy, 2021

"I suggested Ange and I each create some *Lost in Space* art for this book. She's developed into a really fine artist. My stuff still looks like the comic books I made on the set back when I was 12!"
BILL

'The Ghost of Irwin Allen'
Angela Cartwright, 2021

"I'm not a caricature artist. I'd like to be but when I try too hard I'm never happy with the result. But if I let the muse move me, I've learned to accept the outcome and not take myself too seriously. Bill's art really looks like the essence of our cast. I don't really know who these people are in my art piece, but they are the soul of my 'lost in space' family to me. It's curious that Irwin decided to make an appearance without me planning to put him there. Going with those surprises just feels right."
ANGELA

WILL POWER

"It's no secret that I loved creating the original role of Will Robinson. Some characters stick with you and somehow, they become a part of your inner true self. To a certain degree, I believe that has been the case with me and Will.

Once I initially read the pilot script for the new Netflix series Lost in Space, I loved it. Kevin Burns and Jon Jashni had spent years defining the tone and direction they wanted to see the franchise go forward in and they assembled a fantastic team to bring it to reality. I thought the tone was perfect. It harkened back to Irwin Allen's original concept, the same serious attitude that I had tried my best to instill in all the Lost in Space comic books I had written. Plus, it was packed with action, drama, and danger while always retaining a strong sense of an impressive family.

The Will Robinson in the new series was quite different from mine and I was curious to see how the role would be cast. When I heard that Maxwell Jenkins had booked the part, I contacted Joe Straczynski, the creator-writer-executive producer of Babylon 5 (an impressive television series I co-starred in for five years), because I knew Max had worked for Joe on his recent Sense 8 sci-fi series. Joe gave Max a rave review and as usual, he was absolutely right.

Maxwell Jenkins is one of the most impressive and nicest guys I've ever met. He's a very fine and dedicated, enthusiastic actor. Passing the 'Will torch' to him was a true honor. You couldn't ask for a better young man to play the role. Max is a genuinely sweet, kind-hearted, generous, engaged, prepared, interested, capable actor. Being aboard the Jupiter 2 was like going home. Max was the very first cast member I met and we hit it off and connected immediately. I was literally stunned when I discovered that we had so many things in common. Like me when I was his age, Max is a musician and a songwriter. He plays mandolin and guitar... like I did and do. He has a band, like I did and do. Also like me, Max is a huge comic book collector, and his favorite character was Captain America. I told him that back in the day I had modeled the classic Will Robinson on Cap's young partner, Bucky Barnes (nowadays better known as the Winter Soldier). He was blown away by that. While in Vancouver on a weekend, I hiked up to a cool comic book store and bought Max some collected vintage Captain America and Bucky books as well as the Winter Soldier graphic novel.

That week between onstage acting, Max was writing a school report on Pete Seeger, who was a huge influence on me musically back when I was filming Lost In Space in the 1960s. That was yet another subject we had in common.

Bill Mumy Collection

As soon as I got back home to Laurel Canyon in Los Angeles, I made Max a mix of rare Pete Seeger recordings. We were both blown away by the many commonalities we shared beyond just the Robots, spacesuits, and the Robinson name. Max and his wonderful family (sister Samantha, mom Julie, and father Jeff) have been to dinner at my house, we've gone out to restaurants together, we speak often on the phone, we share music and showbiz stories and I'm grateful to say I'm lucky to call them true friends.
All it takes is some Will Power."
BILL

Photos from the Bill Mumy Collection

Will and Will

"For the Netflix-Fox dvd release of Season 1 of the new *Lost In Space* series, working with Max was a blast. I wrote a few scenes that he and I acted together in as both 'Max and Bill' and as 'Will and Will.'
Getting into the classic Will Robinson bright purple velour wardrobe alongside the classic B-9 Robot and filming with Max in his modern Will Robinson spacesuit wardrobe with the new alien Robot was so much fun. We also jammed on mandolins together performing the John Williams Season 3 *Lost in Space* theme. No danger there."
BILL

Photos from Bill Mumy Collection

Meeting the New Robinson Family

Left to right: Angela, Bill, Mina Sundwall, Parker Posey, Maxwell Jenkins, Mark Goddard, Ignacio Serricchio, Marta Kristen.

"Kevin was thrilled to organize a meeting of the Robinsons and he did it the way he knew best... over a family-style meal. It was time to pass the baton to a new Penny. Mina was written some spunky dialog that the Penny of my day could only dream about. That night kicked off a new generation of Robinsons, and everyone was excited for what was ahead."
ANGELA

Photos from Cartwright/Mumy Collections

Danger Will Robinson!

"When I was cast as the real Dr. Smith it was a big secret that Netflix, Legendary, and Synthesis wanted to keep under a tight lid until the new show debuted on the air. It was my idea and I was happy that it worked out. After reading the pilot script and seeing that very small but hugely significant part, I contacted the producers myself and told them that I didn't know if they wanted the classic show to have anything at all to do with their new production, but if they did, I would love to play the part of the real Dr. Smith. I explained to them that I felt it would be a good way to show the die-hard fans of the old series that the new series was embraced, supported, and approved by me. I would be acting as an Ambassador of Good Will (pun intended) and that for me personally, it would resonate as a tribute to the late, great Jonathan Harris.

Bill with Parker Posey.

I was certain Jonathan would say; 'If you can't get ME, then by all means get Billy Person!' They embraced my proposal and it worked out.

When I arrived in Vancouver, a city I dearly dig, I was greeted with open arms. Zack Estrin, the executive producer and showrunner is a wonderful guy, but I found that everyone connected to the project, from the drivers to the wardrobe team, makeup, production assistants, crew members, cast, and producers were all upbeat, positive, happy, excited, and they treated me like royalty."
BILL

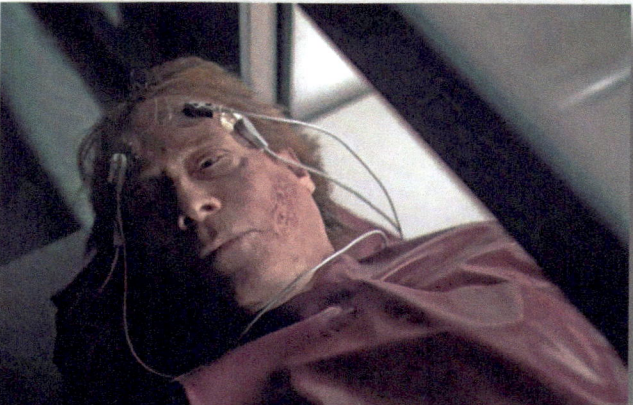

HERE'S TO YOU, MRS. HARRIS!

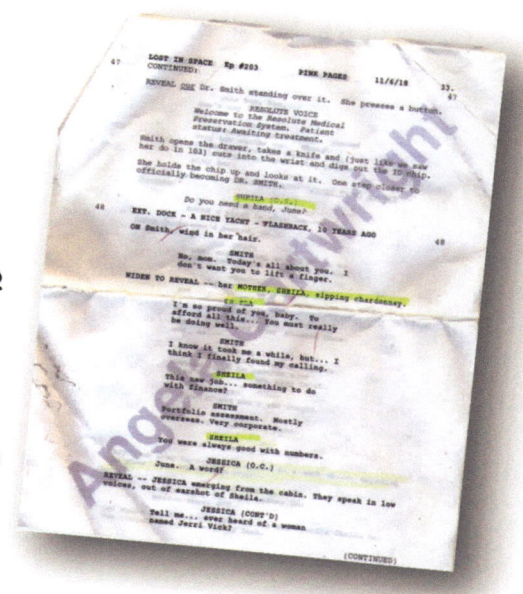

"Kevin was bubbling with excitement when he called me on the phone 'Angelinio?' (Only Kevin and Jonathan have called me that!) 'Guess what?! You are going to be in Season 2 of the Netflix *Lost In Space* and you are going to play Sheila Harris!' Kevin got a huge kick out of the play on names and was thrilled to have the classic cast be in this amazing reboot, not just as a cameo, but as an important part of the evolving story.

I was the nasty dying mother of June (Parker Posey) and Jessica (Selma Blair), the catalyst to the storyline which led to some of Dr. Smith's evil ways.

As Bill said, the cast and crew were great to work with, and I had a blast freezing my butt off in the Canadian winter while sipping a faux martini on a boat."
ANGELA

Angela with Selma Blair.

Premiere Fun!

Premiere of the Netflix *Lost In Space*
Cinerama Dome
April 9, 2018
Angela and Bill with Ignacio Serricchio, Parker Posey, and Maxwell Jenkins.

Photos from Cartwright/Mumy Collections

"It was a red carpet affair at the Cinerama Dome in Los Angeles to show the first two episodes of the new *Lost In Space* series. Needless to say the effects were light-years better than our classic ones and I loved Penny's spunk. She was able to be more vocal than 50 years ago. All in all it was a wonderful night and the afterparty was a galactic blast."
ANGELA

The Road to Conventions

"To many people the thought of traveling to new locations around the world is a very appealing subject. I understand that. And of course, the thought of being fawned over and stroked by thousands of adoring fans who flock to tickle your ego and collect your autograph sounds like fun. However, flying to and attending conventions isn't always sunshine and lollipops. It can be quite another thing.

I've been attending science fiction, comic book, fantasy, and autograph shows for over 40 years now. Sometimes, they are wonderful. Sometimes they are not.

What they often are is: long drives to airports, waiting for delayed flights, being bounced around in turbulence, then landing and waiting for luggage and wondering why yours had to be the one suitcase they lost, and hoping the ride that was scheduled to pick you up is actually there waiting to pick you up. Calling to find out that it's 'on its way' which can mean sitting outside on a bench, in the snow, staring at every van that drives past the airport gate to see if your name is in the window. If it is, a long drive is usually ahead to a hotel that involves registering and credit cards you didn't want to use. Then with little sleep there are long days sitting at tables, wearing your best smile, and putting on your kindest and coolest attitude, answering questions you've answered a thousand times before, like you're answering them for the first time. Then before you know it, everything is quickly thrown into reverse mode and you do it all again backwards to get back home to your family and your other projects.

Photos by Steve Gullion

Sightseeing and the opportunity to take in local culture happens occasionally, but it's rare. Meeting and greeting and signing and posing with fans from 9:00 in the morning till 7:00 in the evening can be exhausting. You want people to have a positive experience encountering you. You share appreciation, trips down memory lane, and put out good vibes to make sure people go away pleased. Sometimes it's exactly like acting on camera. Sometimes it's tough and usually when the workday is over, the opportunity to go out to a recommended restaurant quite a distance away from the hotel with fans for an extended evening of talking is just too much. Normally, I choose to retreat to my hotel room and have an overpriced room service meal delivered. Trust me, ordering clam chowder in Phoenix in July was a huge mistake! There's nothing pleasant about getting a dose of severe food poisoning from bad room service.

More than a few winter storms have delayed or cancelled flights and a night in a plastic chair in an airport awaiting news of a new departure time from a distant gate is no fun. Don't even get me started on the joys of serious air turbulence and problematic planes. I could blow your mind with some tales of emergency landings after being struck by lightning... TWICE! Ahhh, but I'll save those for my own book one day (ha!).

Ange has a trick of putting Neosporin in your nostrils before boarding planes to act as a filtration aid, but that doesn't do any good when the plane is violently bouncing up and down through a storm like a bear with its head stuck in a bucket of honey.

I can't tell you very much about all the various global locations I've been to attending conventions over the years. Sure, a brisk walk along the foggy coast in England, a great pizza in Atlanta, a stroll in the snow at Christmas in Ohio, a few beers with the cast at the Samuel Adams brewery in Boston... those are memorable sweet moments. But there were also many fire alarms going off in the middle of the night where we've been forced to evacuate the hotel and stand outside in the rain while the authorities take their time to confirm a drunken fan set off the alarm.

Back before the world was struggling to survive a global pandemic, there were still contagious germs being spread around at conventions. People want to hug you. People want to kiss you. People want to shake your hand. People hand you things to sign with their pens and people cough in your face. I've gotten quite sick multiple times from convention experiences. While we were attending the Hollywood Show in 2015 celebrating the 50th anniversary of the series, June was with us. She was a real trouper and was the first one set up every morning and the last to break down at the end of the day. She was also 89 years old then and she caught the flu from a fan. That was her last convention. She has wisely chosen not to risk it further. So, although the allure and glamour of 'celebrity' can indeed shine bright to those looking at it from the outside, it can also be a dark place at times.

All in all, it's been totally worth it."
BILL

Photos from Cartwright/Mumy Collections

CONTACT 96 - Disney World 1996.

MegaCon - Orlando, Florida 1992.

Hollywood Show - Los Angeles, California 2011.

ScoutCon - Tampa, Florida 2008.

Hollywood Show - Los Angeles, California 2011.

Hollywood Show - Los Angeles, California 2006.

Photos: from CartwrightMumy Collections

StarCon - Pasadena, California 1997.

Hollywood Show - Los Angeles, California 2018.

Chiller Convention - New Jersey 2015.

"Not the real chariot but an amazing replica built on a Sno-Cat body. The fans really enjoyed checking it out."
ANGELA

Steve Gullion with Angela and Bill, In an airport somewhere in the USA 2018.

Photos: from Cartwright/Mumy Collections

Hollywood Show - Chicago, Illinois 2012.

Photos from Cartwright/Mumy Collections

"I've signed spaceships and robots, helmets, lunchboxes, and baseballs, but the craziest thing I have ever been asked to sign at a convention would have to be Guy Williams' jockstrap connected to his green velour shirt. That was plain weird. This picture above was taken at the last convention we attended with June. The end of an era."
ANGELA

ALIEN CON

Photos from Cartwright/Mumy Collections

Alien Con - Santa Clara, California 2016.

"Alien Con was the brain child of Kevin Burns, hot off the success of *Ancient Aliens*, which Bill was a producer on for four seasons. The Alien Con events were a huge success. The first one was in 2016 up north and then in 2018 some of the cast of the new and the classic *Lost In Space* were invited. But the real stars were the speakers discussing alien discoveries, a subject the thousands of people attending couldn't get enough of." ANGELA

Alien Con panel - Santa Clara, California - 2016   Jon Jashni, Bill, Mark, Angela, Marta, and Kevin Burns.

Alien Con - Pasadena, California 2018.

Two Pennys, Two Wills.

Photos from Cartwright/Mumy Collections

ODE TO KEVIN

"This isn't the proper place to write Kevin Burns' eulogy. Kevin was a brilliant, generous, complicated, loyal, multi-talented, enthusiastic man and a great friend to us. Know this: if not for the tireless and never-ending love, vision, tenacity, and support that Kevin Burns had for *Lost in Space*, literally none of the projects that included those three words in the past 30+ years would ever have happened.
Rest in Peace, Kevbo, and thank you kindly."
BILL & ANGELA

Photos from Cartwright/Mumy Collections

Photo by Eileen Mumy

Photos from Cartwright/Mumy Collections

"The picture above was the last time we saw Kevin. It was Marta's birthday celebration and like all meals we had with Kevin there were laughs, monologues, memories, and stories. The get-togethers were a couple times a year and they always had a family roundtable vibe. I'll miss them, but it's Kevin I'll miss the most."
ANGELA

Candid Photos from Cartwright/Mumy Collections

KEVIN BURNS

Born: June 18, 1955, Schenectady, NY
Died: September 27, 2020, Los Angeles, CA

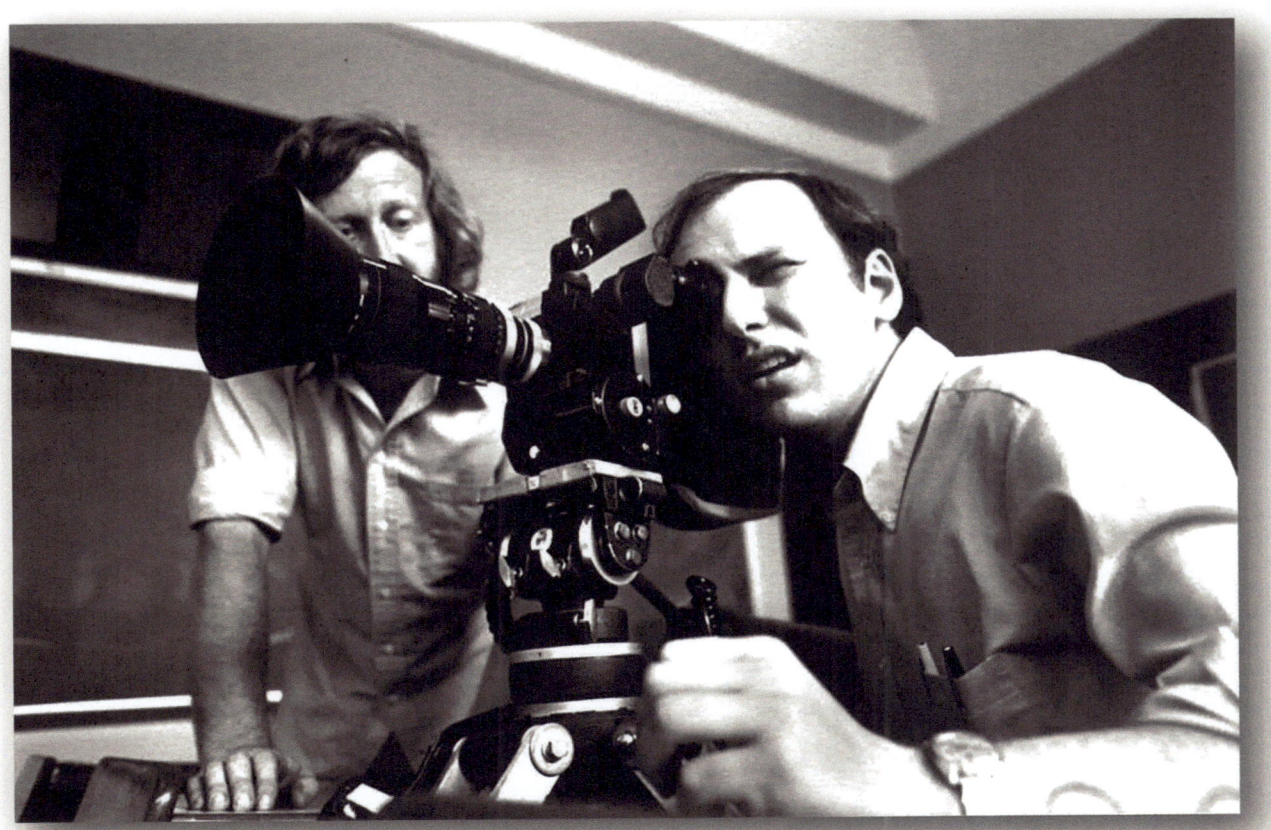

FYI After winning a student Academy Award for his documentary *I Remember Barbra*, Kevin moved to Hollywood and never stopped working. In addition to his legacy of Irwin Allen productions, Kevin was widely recognized as a prolific Emmy-winning producer of the classic A&E *Biography* series, the long-running History Channel series *Ancient Aliens*, and so much more. Kevin's portfolio included over 800 hours of wide-ranging television content including *The Girls Next Door*, *Food Paradise*, *The UnXplained with William Shatner*, and *The Curse of Oak Island*, just to name a few.

We've Been Friends For So Long Now...

Photos from Cartwright/Mumy Collections

"Having been asked by our publishers to ruminate on and write something about the relationship between me and Angela, I realize what a deep, unique, and multi-faceted thing our relationship is. Over the course of 57 years Angela and I have been children in school together for several years, with no other students but each other to relate to. We share the rarity of having grown up in professional showbiz and having been 'child stars' together and carrying that title (and the weight that comes with it) ever since. We have both known the responsibility of almost daily work as very young children and we have both come through that experience relatively unscathed.
We have been professional co-workers in television, radio, print, film, music, art, photography, and personal appearances.
We've been friends and we've been more than friends.
We have been estranged and we have been reunited.
We have supported each other's projects and we have had disagreements.
We have been colleagues and cheerleaders.
We have been there for each other when our friends have passed, and our parents have died. We knew them all quite well.
We have been traveling companions.
We have seen each other's long successful 40+ years of marriage thrive and maneuver over some rough times.
We have watched each other become parents and now grandparents.
We have pretty much been everything together."
BILL

Photos by John V. Cartwright

Photos from Cartwright/Mumy Collections

So Long, Farewell... The Last Chapter

We've gotten used to returning to *Lost in Space* one way or another after believing that it would 'never happen again' multiple times now, so we won't definitively say this time it's a final wrap... but it might be.

There were so many important *Lost in Space* major events that manifested into reality after we completed the first edition of this book, *Lost (and) Found In Space*, that we both truly felt that creating this updated, expanded, and revised version was a worthy and necessary project.

Discovering a huge cache of unseen vintage photographs, getting together, and celebrating the show's history with our 'classic' castmates for television, radio, internet, and personal appearances, and being a part of the ambitious and wonderful 21st century Netflix series and enjoying how fans of the classic show also embraced the Netflix series has been truly rewarding in many ways.

However, with the sad realities of the passing of Kevin Burns and the Covid global pandemic, it makes us feel like we may very well have taken our final encore bows this time. But one thing's for sure, we're sure of nothing. Should the opportunity present itself... we are still here.
Co-creating both volumes of this book have been true labors of love.

Indeed.

Thank you kindly, and cheers.

Billy Mumy stars as Will Robinson in Twentieth Television's "Lost In Space."

About the Authors

Angela Cartwright - artist, actress, author, photographer, designer, entrepreneur, curator, art instructor, voice-over artist, wife, mother, and grandmother, not always in that order...

Angela was born in Cheshire, England and moved to Los Angeles, California with her family and immediately started to work as a child fashion model. Angela's career in front of the camera started at age three and includes many iconic acting roles including *The Danny Thomas Show* for seven seasons, the legendary movie *The Sound of Music* as Brigitta, and the iconic television show *Lost In Space* as Penny Robinson where she first worked with Bill Mumy.

She has collaborated on and authored eight books including *The Sound of Music Family Scrapbook* and the award-winning *Styling The Stars: Lost Treasures from the Twentieth Century Fox Archive*, which offers never-before-seen photographs and a behind the scenes exclusive glimpse inside the 20th Century Fox Archive.

Angela's mixed media art is collected around the world and she has pioneered and produced a clothing and jewelry line.

She enjoys her children and grandchildren and makes her home in California with her husband Steve. Angela has found her purpose is to love, laugh, and always create.

angela-cartwright.com   angelacartwrightstudio.com

Bill Mumy is an actor, songwriter, recording artist, producer, voice-over artist, musician, photographer, husband, father, grandfather, and worry wart.

Entering the arena of professional entertainment at the age of five, Bill has worked on over 400 television shows and is best known by fans around the world for the creation of his memorable roles as the heroic boy astronaut Will Robinson on the long-running classic series *Lost in Space*, Anthony Fremont from *The Twilight Zone,* and Lennier from the popular science fiction series *Babylon 5*, which he co-starred in for five years.

Bill has written scores of comic books and television shows, in addition to collaborating with his *Lost in Space* co-star Angela Cartwright on two previous books. He also served as a consulting producer on the long-running hit television series *Ancient Aliens*.

Mumy is a prolific songwriter and recording artist, with numerous solo cds, as well as being half of the infamous novelty rock recording and short film making duo Barnes and Barnes, best known for the classic demented song and film *Fish Heads*. He has also worked with the pop group America off and on for over 30 years, composing, producing, and performing with the band.

Bill has two grown children, and two adorable granddaughters, upon whom he dotes. He lives in the Hollywood Hills of California with his wife, Eileen.

billmumy.com

Thanks to our families, those here and those gone and those yet to come, who travel with us on our journeys into the past and always pull us back to reality when we get lost in space.

Angela Cartwright Collection

Thanks to all the talented, good people who worked alongside us in front of and behind the cameras, our castmates and crewmates from over the years. Thanks to everyone who watched, listened, and read, with a special nod to Ron Nastrom, Ron Hamill, Carl Guido, and Perry Corvese.
Our thanks goes to Irwin and Sheila Allen, Jon Jashni, Derek Thielges, Derek Shimoda, and Deborah Herman; John and Margaret Cartwright and Muriel Mumy for the additional behind the scenes photography; and Steve, Jesse, Eileen, and Tom for capturing the extra candid moments.
Many thanks to Next Chapter Publishing's Mary and Tom McLaren for their many attributes and wise counsel.
And a very special thanks to Kevin Burns without whom none of this would have been possible.